Co-Creating

Co-Creating
A Feminist Vision of Ministry

Lynn N. Rhodes

The Westminster Press
Philadelphia

Scripture quotations from the Revised Standard Version of the Bible are copyrighted 1946, 1952, © 1971, 1973 by the Division of Christian Education of the National Council of the Churches of Christ in the U.S.A. and are used by permission.

Quotations marked NEB are from *The New English Bible.* © The Delegates of the Oxford University Press and The Syndics of the Cambridge University Press 1961, 1970. Used by permission.

"in answer to your silly question" by Alice Walker from *Goodnight, Willie Lee, I'll See You in the Morning.* Copyright © 1975, 1977, 1979 by Alice Walker. Reprinted by permission of Doubleday & Company, Inc.

Book design by Gene Harris

First edition

Published by The Westminster Press®
Philadelphia, Pennsylvania

PRINTED IN THE UNITED STATES OF AMERICA

9 8 7 6 5 4 3 2 1

Library of Congress Cataloging-in-Publication Data

Rhodes, Lynn N., 1943–
Co-creating : a feminist vision of ministry.

   Originally presented as the author's thesis (doctoral).
   1. Pastoral theology. 2. Women clergy.
3. Feminism—Religious aspects—Christianity.
I. Title.
BV4011.R52 1987   253'.088042   87-10518
ISBN 0-664-24032-1 (pbk.)

Contents

77068

*I am unusually blessed by friends
who have become family
and a family who are my friends.
From you I have learned what I know
of solidarity and of friendship.*

Preface

I began the research for this book when I realized that women who have struggled over the past twenty years or more as local church clergy and who have maintained a commitment to justice for women have few opportunities to share their feminist vision and insights into present forms of ministry. They are involved in the daily concerns of people and they are attempting to evoke personal and systemic change in a sexist and patriarchal system. I wanted to discover what they have learned and what they share in common with women who are writing feminist theology. Out of the interaction of theory and practice, what vision for church life is emerging? I wanted to make visible the wisdom and imagination of women who care passionately about the future possibilities of women and who work to make that vision concrete.

As a clergywoman I know the fear of co-optation, and as a seminary teacher I have moments of great doubt as to the effectiveness of my work. I share with others a dissatisfaction with how we are preparing women and men for the ministry of the churches. Yet I believe that feminists are developing perspectives and actions that can reshape theological education and our concepts of ministry. I hope and work for the time when feminist insights will be incorporated into new visions of love and justice and new hope for all of creation.

The movements for liberation have formed and informed my work in the church. The civil rights movement brought me up against my participation in racist structures and my internalized prejudice. It also gave me a glimpse into the empowerment that comes when people "name themselves" and refuse to be victims. I have learned from the antiwar movement and the present peace movements about the terrible urgency to find ways to stop nuclear madness. I have found great joy, energy, and life's work with sisters in the feminist movement. These have been not only "movements" but communities of friends, vision and nourishment.

In the course of my work I have been constantly astonished at the spirit of women who will not be daunted by the enormity of the tasks. They are not blind to the evil and pain of this world. They just refuse to let that be the last word or the last action.

Here is the result of the willingness of women to share their stories and their visions with me. I have, of course, interpreted what they have told me within my own particular frames of reference and experience. Nonetheless, this book literally could not have been written without them.

The book comes out of my work as a student and as a seminary field educator. Robert Treese, my colleague in field education, first urged me to think about writing down my concerns. He is a true friend who always respected my work and who knows no way to be in relationship, except in mutuality. My other colleagues, Linda Clark and Jim Fraser, made the system work for me. Mary Pellauer, Nancy Adess, and Linda Clark helped move this material from dissertation to book form. They also know how to critique and support at the right moments. Brinton Lykes has been a constant friend who reminds me of what solidarity is about. She, Nancy Richardson,

Carol Robb, Glenda Hope, and Ruth Smith have helped me be accountable to relationship, justice, and ethical sensitivity.

The women who most shaped this book are the women clergy who live this ministry and do not give up hope: Alice Hageman, Elizabeth Rice, Sally Dyck, Donna Day-Lower, Odette Lockwood-Stewart, Fay Ellison, Patricia Farris, Donna Atkinson, Kathy M. Young, Helen Neinast, Donna Schaper, Dee Crabtree, Phyllis Tyler Wayman, and Bonnie Jones-Goldstein.

To new friends along the way who typed, retyped, and still kept a sense of humor about it all, go my thanks: to Becky Jones, Paul Crego, Dianne Strickert, and Craig Hall Cutting.

Feminists who care about justice and the well-being of all women have my great respect. They are companions of the soul who feed me when I'm sick, urge me to one more protest action, and continue to practice steadfastness and compassion. They strengthen my desire to be about the building of a new creation.

1

Why Feminist Ministry?

This book addresses the insights of a particular group of women: feminists in Christian ministry. They are women who are developing a vision of Christianity that cares passionately about the well-being, the full dignity, and the humanity of all women. I have examined how these women are interpreting the meaning of authority, salvation, mission, and vocation as they carry out their work and develop their theory. This is not a systematic or comprehensive survey of Christian theology, but an examination of issues central to a Christian feminist vision of ministry.

I have chosen to work with feminists who identify themselves within the liberation movements of Christianity. As feminists they are clear that sexism is a reality for all women but that it functions differently for white middle-class women, women of color, and women in different cultures and class systems. As feminists they seek to expose sexism and struggle for the well-being of women. As women committed to liberation, they seek to address sexism in the context of race, class, and nation. Justice is the ethical norm. The insights of oppressed groups are essential to understanding the content and context of justice anywhere. Furthermore, this feminist perspective finds injustice and the resulting lack of mutuality to be endemic in our present cultural, social, and religious institutions. Therefore, the basic task is to seek understanding of the causes of injustice in every situation in order to resist oppression and foster liberation.

Of course, the challenge of injustice is not a task for women alone. We all need to confront the implications of sexism because, as Beverly Wildung Harrison, the Christian social ethicist, states:

> We all need a recovery of our full, integrated humanity. . . . Feminism is a call to genuine strength in women *and* men, a strength born of the power of relationship. Active love and passion for justice sends our roots deep, to discover or recover our connections with all that is. Such shared strength does enable us to keep faith, and we need that strength, for our faith calls us to ongoing, difficult, and challenging work.[1]

This book draws mainly on two contemporary resources: white women clergy and theologians who, with a few exceptions, work in and are from mainline Protestant denominations in the United States. As they work within church institutions, they acknowledge that the struggle to live out the implications of feminism are difficult. Some say it is impossible. Yet these women continue vocationally to struggle with ambiguity, pain, and the dangers of co-optation. They make such efforts as long as they can find ways to nourish, sustain, and broaden visions.

In the early years of the present women's movement, women spent enormous energy in defending and justifying their place in church leadership and in seeking ordination. They learned to negotiate the tricky issues "when the minister is a woman" (as one early book was titled) and to show that they could handle the work. As more women became ordained, the issues for many feminists shifted from gaining acceptance to critiquing the institution itself. Now more and more women are moving to create new forms of ministry. Some of these forms are external to the present mainline church structures (Women-Church being one such effort), and others are emerging from within present structures. It is this constructive task of developing feminist interpretations of ministry that I am addressing here.

This book is first of all for women who are attempting to incorporate their feminist insights into their work as clergy in Christian ministry. Within the daily struggle to respond to issues of people's lives, to attend to individual pain and need and organize committee meetings, prepare worship services, counsel, and teach, it is often hard to keep sight of the vision and reflect upon experiences. Thus it is crucial for feminists to articulate vision, both to keep our passion for ministry alive and to help hold ourselves accountable to the deepest beliefs we profess and confess. Most of us are informed and shaped by the subtle and not-so-subtle rationales of the systems and institutions that dominate our lives. If we wish not to be co-opted by the patriarchal church, we need to articulate our values and incorporate them into the structures of our communities. Otherwise, we will soon lose our vision or become so alienated that we will need to leave the church as an institution in order to maintain our commitments and our integrity.

We who have begun to take on leadership functions in the church have a further consideration—not to perpetuate forms of power over others that diminish or oppress any other group. As a white, educated woman, I am conscious that I continue to operate out of my own ethnic and class assumptions. By articulating feminist values and suggesting some implications for ministry that they imply, I hope to provide a forum where we can be held accountable and be challenged to continue to reformulate practice in light of our commitment to end all forms of oppression.

Reflections on feminist ministry are also crucial for
the life of the whole church. We are becoming in-
creasingly aware of the extensiveness of sexist practices in the church and the culture. During the last
fifteen years, feminist theologians have accom-
plished much in exploring the meaning of sexism.
They have uncovered the history of what has denied,
diminished, and distorted the expression of the full
humanity of women in the church. They have begun
to unearth and to interpret women's religious experiences. And they have explored feminist perspectives
on the meaning of the Christian faith and mission.
The work of feminists, and the thought of liberation-
ists generally, has helped us realize that Christian
theology has been developed by a relatively small
group of people—mostly men, mostly white, mostly
from European–North American culture. Yet the
sexist practices of the church are multi-layered and
widespread. Many churches are still resisting women
as pastors, the use of inclusive language, and changes
in family roles. Churches need to be continually challenged by a theory and practice of ministry that does
not discriminate against women and does not exploit
ethnic or racial groups.

Furthermore, whether or not churches explicitly
challenge sexism, they are still going to be confronted with new issues as women explore their own
faith. The recent influx of women into theological
education and professional ministries raises new
questions and concerns about family and child care,
the relationship between female and male colleagues, authority, traditional symbols and images of
the holy, and the meaning of sexuality. These questions cannot be silenced. We hope they will be seen
as opening up new possibilities for church life. A
feminist view is essential to forwarding our treat-
ment of these concerns.

Even more, feminist perspectives on ministry can
provide some crucial ingredients for thinking about

other issues in ministry. In the 1950s, H. Richard Niebuhr noted that people in the church and the seminaries were very unclear about the purpose and meaning of ministry. He called the ordained clergy the "perplexed profession." He also predicted that a new consensus about the role of clergy was developing.[2] In fact, that consensus never emerged. In recent writings about ministry, clergy continue to express anxiety about their role in society and the functions they should perform in the church. One of the major issues continues to center around the roles and identities of clergy and laity. We still have not satisfactorily addressed the Protestant ideal of the priesthood of all believers. While affirming the ministry of the whole church, we are still practicing a ministry that is largely seen as carried out by clergy.

The rise of liberation movements, our growing awareness of diverse Christian religious practices and beliefs, and our encounters with different racial and cultural traditions may make the clergy even more "perplexed" today than in the 1950s. More aware than before of the cultural and class biases that we have incorporated into the practice of ministry, clergy may desperately need insights showing them how to deal with such questions in the life of the church.

It is also important to understand the implications of feminist visions of ministry in relation to religion and public life. In the last century, Protestant domination of American culture has lessened. As a result, much of the work of the ordained clergy has been relegated to the margins of public life and political leadership. Clergy have been doing work associated more generally with the individual, the family, and private life—dealing with the personal pains and needs of people. They have been connected to the tasks and sensitivities that have been traditionally assigned to women, such as nurturance, service functions, and spiritual concerns.[3] In a society where women's work is politically and economically marginalized, the church can be seen as fulfilling traditional feminine roles. There is a fear expressed by some that if women enter the ordained ministry in large numbers, men will leave it, thus making a "feminized" organization all female. This will be seen as a threat as long as we associate female with the private sphere of life and male with the public and political issues of life.

These concerns are central to feminism. "The personal is political" is a basic tenet of today's women's movement. Feminists are strongly committed to overcoming the split between privatized religion or personalized caring and social policy or social change. Feminists have named the issue of private and public life in a way that opens new avenues for dealing with it. They have begun to experiment with some strategies that may be helpful. Their work provides clues for all of us in the church to investigate and explore further on this subject.

To set this book within the context of current discussions on ministry in the major, predominantly white middle-class Protestant denominations, I will briefly outline some current trends in writing about ministry. Each of these categories emphasizes a particular concern, and most focus on clergy. The categories do not encompass all issues, nor are they intended to suggest that any one category excludes the others. They do give us a context for the preoccupations and concerns of many who work in churches.

The first category I have labeled the *arts and skills of professional church leadership.* The concern is to describe the necessary arts and skills that make the present leadership effective and professional so that the church can be clear about accountability and evaluation. The intent is to help clergy develop effective skills and choose the appropriate standards for job performance, as well as to provide a framework for professional standards of training, accreditation, and behavior. The concern is to describe what clergy actually do and to understand what the church expects of its trained leadership. Much material on ministry reflects this concern for competency, skill training, and assessment of personality traits needed for professional leadership.[4]

A second category of literature on ministry focuses on *personhood*. In this material the concern is on the quality of personal relationship to self, others, and God. The essence of ministry is not skill development or structure, but relationship. Much of the pastoral care movement, with its emphasis on psychological insight and healing ministry, comes under this category. The issue for church life centers in the ability of people to deepen their own spiritual life and to learn to respond to one another out of their own humanity. One of the most powerful images to emerge from this approach is that of "wounded healer," which came from a book of the same title by theologian Henri Nouwen.[5]

A third category is *ministry of office and order*. Writers in this field examine the tradition of, and biblical foundations for, the historical validity of the offices of ministry. The clergy are set apart as "representatives" who administer the sacraments, order church life, and interpret scripture. The special calling of clergy is centered in their sacramental and representative work. The sacraments embody the vision and continuity of the church and preserve the integrity of the historical faith. Clergy are entrusted with the task of calling the church to its service in the world. Ordination is a sign of the people's trust that the clergy will carry out with faithfulness the church's intent over the years. Although this perspective is most evident in the Roman Catholic and Episcopalian traditions, it is a major component of almost all rationales for ordination.[6]

Ministry organized contextually and defined by its vision is the fourth category. The essential character-

istics of ministry are defined by the church's understanding of how it incorporates its vision within historical contexts. Ministry forms and leadership roles
address the political, social, and religious needs of a
particular situation. As it articulates its vision, the
church can evaluate and determine the shape of its
sense of mission and thus its particular role in the
world. Ministry oriented toward mission has most
recently been the concern of liberation theologians.
Ministry models are shaped as people address particular contexts in light of their analysis of God's intent
for the world.[7]

Much of the evidence reviewed in the rest of this
book suggests that feminist theories are most closely
aligned with the fourth category, although feminists
are also concerned about skills, individual development, care, and ritual. A feminist clergywoman
whose basic approach is in the fourth category still
needs to administer, communicate, counsel, and educate. She needs resources to help her develop skills
in specific functions, and she needs to learn how to
establish modes of accountability. She also has a
strong and abiding sense of the central importance of
personhood, which feminism emphasizes and which
fuels her concern for the specific people in the context in which she works. She is very much aware of
the power of ritual and sacrament and finds them to
be deeply nurturing sources of community life and
its sustenance. Yet the emphasis of this book is on
context and vision; on what feminists have learned
from their encounter with sexism as expressed in the
political, social, and religious communities; and on
what they envision will enhance the well-being and
full humanity of women. Thus, models of ministry
are developed out of a critique of patriarchy and out
of experiences of what liberates and nourishes
women.

I have examined the work of feminist theologians,
especially that of Letty M. Russell, Beverly Wildung

Harrison, and Rosemary Radford Ruether. They have been critical theorists for women struggling with sexism and patriarchal religion. They also share a common commitment to addressing Christianity from a feminist liberation perspective.

Letty Russell worked for many years as a pastor in the multiracial East Harlem Protestant Parish. She has been active in the ecumenical movement. Her theory arises from her pastoral, educational, and ecumenical concerns. Her recent focus on the concept of partnership in ministry has been important for many clergywomen.

Beverly Wildung Harrison is one of the major feminist theorists in religious social ethics. She has consistently addressed concrete issues of moral life. She has written on the ethics of abortion and published a collection of essays that covers an enormous range of critical contemporary ethical issues.

Rosemary Radford Ruether has published numerous books and articles on feminism, liberation, and Christian theology. She has been influential in a wide variety of areas, addressing sexism, racism, and anti-Semitism as well as developing new nonsexist interpretations of Christianity.

Along with these feminist theologians, I have been informed by the wider feminist and liberation movements because their work has been integral to our commitment to liberation and spiritual awakening.

The second group that has provided material for this book are clergywomen who are pastors in local churches. The insights and themes explored here about feminist visions of ministry have been developed over two decades of dialogue with many women with whom I have learned, ministered, taught, and grown. I cannot number or name all these friends, acquaintances, teachers, and colleagues.

However, for this book I have interviewed fourteen clergywomen in some depth about their work.

I make no claim that they are a representative cross section such as sociological surveys are based on. I have chosen to pursue some questions in detail with a small number of clergywomen. But the experiences and stories of many other women not interviewed formally certainly inform this work. The women I chose to interview were selected for a number of reasons. They all have had considerable experience as local church pastors, with service ranging from ten to thirty years as ordained clergy. They are from mainline Protestant churches and share certain characteristics in their approach to ministry. They are white women attempting consciously to develop feminist ministries and trying to confront issues of race and class. They share a deep commitment to a kind of feminism that insists upon struggles on behalf of all women, and that therefore necessitates connecting struggles against sexism with those against racism, economic oppression, and war.

These clergywomen, like the feminist theologians, have worked on many issues of injustice. Their work experiences include organizing women's shelters with multi-ethnic women's groups, community organizing with rural and urban youth, antiwar and nuclear disarmament support, and organizing around issues of abortion, racism, prisons, and women's centers. All have been informed by the liberation, antiwar, and feminist movements. They have been active in feminist caucuses and organizations, both within and without church structures. Some of the women have had experiences in other countries, including Third World countries. Most have been active in, or supportive of, liberation movements in South Africa, South America, and other places.

Most of these women have been involved in church activities all their lives. The local church was often the arena for their own leadership development and consciousness-raising as they were growing up. Many had encountered one or more important female models, for example, a youth leader or a relative.

Their life experience is varied. They are single, married, widowed, or divorced. Some have children or stepchildren. Their parish positions include primary pastor, co-pastor, one of a clergy couple, one of a multiple staff team, and associate pastor. Their parishes include rural, suburban, urban, and small-town churches, with people from low to high income ranges, and with diverse ethnic groups.

All these women encountered discrimination against women in institutions and attitudes. For many, the most intense experiences of sexism occurred in seminary. All have been active leaders in feminist concerns and organizations. All have been the token female in male-dominated organizations. Some expressed having a sense of entitlement (a phrase used by one to indicate an early expectation due in part to class and race, that their lives would be significant). Others found it very difficult to develop their own assertiveness and have had to work hard to see their work as important. They are aware of the contradiction between, on the one hand, the inherited "privileges" of race, education, and membership in a "First World" country that give them access to power and, on the other, their subordinate status in a sexist culture and in patriarchal religious institutions.

These women express a great love of their work. "What could be more exciting," said one, "than having a job that allows you to be involved in the totality of people's lives in a community—the drama, richness, sorrow, and joy that you participate in?" Nevertheless, they experience frustrations, weariness, and discouragement that come, they say, from the difficult struggle for liberation and the enormous needs they see expressed in the lives of people. They express passionate commitments to justice and the possibilities for wholeness in people's lives. "You know a lot about me," said one, "when you know my family motto: 'Hurl thunderbolts at evil.'" I have quoted these women in this book but have not identified the specific individuals. I hope I have remained faithful to the intent of their sharing with me, for they were generous with their time and open in their reflections.

Two groups who are not included in this book are particularly significant in the development of feminist theory: ordained women of color and laywomen from all ethnic groups. Ordained women of color have the double burden of sexual and racial discrimination. Laywomen's contribution to the church has been enormous, but has often been relegated to the private sphere and almost totally unrecognized in official church histories. Both groups suffer exclusion from male-dominated churches run by "professional" clergy. It is my hope that the theory developed from the experience of white feminist clergywomen will be helpful in the struggle for liberation of all women. But I recognize that we who are in leadership positions can fail to see our own complicity and need to recognize our limitations. I hope that the articulation of our vision will help hold us accountable to the women whose lives are not recounted in this book.

In weaving together the reflections on feminist ministry from these two groups, feminist clergywomen in the local parish and feminist theologians in seminary education, I have also included sources from feminist and liberation poets and writers who have furthered my insight and sparked my imagination. The central chapters of this book are organized around the reflections of these women upon the following questions.

By what *authority* do these women develop their understanding of ministry, and how do they exercise their own authority? What is their understanding of the message of the Christian story of *salvation?* What is their understanding of the *mission* of the church today? What is their understanding of the meaning of Christian *vocation?*

These major themes are interwoven and interconnected, as we shall see. Understandings of authority underlie definitions of salvation, mission, and vocation, and each interacts with and informs the others.

In struggling to develop affirmations about authority, salvation, mission, and vocation, these feminists also recognize the tensions inherent in relating vision to present lived realities. As they confront the denial of authority to women in the Christian tradition, they struggle to affirm an authority that does not perpetuate dominating or authoritarian roles. As the Christian promise of new creation (salvation) shapes their vision of radical and imaginative change, they also continue to struggle to make God's promises real in concrete ways in the daily lives of people in the local parish. As they act in mission out of particular situations and contexts, they also aim to reach across vast boundaries of oppression or social gaps. While clarifying their own gifts and callings, they find simultaneously that as they participate in the clergy role they are radically questioning it and exploring new directions so as to empower all people more fully.

For these women feminism is much more than a label, an ideology that is "politically correct," or a system to which all feminists must conform. It is an ethical imperative and a process of discernment. Building on each other's work, communicating more deeply, listening carefully to each other about the real pains and joys of ministry, they are challenging each other to go further.

Feminists' understandings of ministry are also a challenge to the whole church to go further. Some of the values and vision we hold are shared by others. The implications for specific models of ministry from a feminist perspective are not necessarily unique. Few of the specific proposals are without some precedent. They do build upon past insights. *What is of critical importance is that we ground our ministry in reflection upon women's experience and in the ethical challenge to care for the well-being of all women and the development of their full humanity.* The women clergy and theologians of this study have staked their lives on the hope and growing wisdom that to be Christian can mean to respond to God's call for a *new* creation where all life is held in mutual regard and where justice is the norm.

In this study, feminist perspectives on ministry set forth a distinctive set of pressures experienced and commitments made by Christian feminists as they struggle to live out and to understand the faith dimensions of their whole lives. There are conflicts and new possibilities about authority, tensions and excitements about what God's promises and works of salvation mean, emerging insights about being missional people, and both obstacles and opportunities for shaping our vocations as Christians today. Out of these pressures and possibilities, feminists ask the whole church to listen, to challenge, and most of all to join in the exploration.

2

By What Authority?

Throughout the history of the church, Christians have struggled over the issue of authority. They have argued, split apart, and even fought wars over the interpretation of scripture and the extent to which tradition, the Holy Spirit, reason, and revelation are authoritative for the guidance and development of the church. Elsie Gibson, writing in 1970 on women ministers, recognized this:

> The locus of authority has been a bone of contention since the first disciples thought Jesus had a spectacular future and vied for the place of honor at his side. It is still unresolved. Jesus contended unsuccessfully with the problem throughout his ministry and was still face to face with it at death. Washing the disciples' feet at the Last Supper was a penultimate attempt to clarify his meaning, but the church has not heard the message in a way to create ideological renewal in its stance on authority, which is still the central cause of division among Christians, a fact which should lead all churches to rethink their position in depth.[1]

For feminists, the usual issues about authority are further complicated by the overarching context of patriarchy—the systemic subordination and devaluing of women throughout the history of Christianity.

It has been men in dominant positions within the Christian tradition who have told the stories, written down their memories of events, and interpreted the meaning of the faith in creeds and institutions. It has been assumed that these perspectives on life's meaning could be generalized. In fact, these interpretations have largely ignored the stories and insights of women. As feminist theologians have shown, women have lacked the power and freedom to participate fully in recording, governing, and interpreting the life of faith communities. Because of this, women have found it difficult to validate their own experiences, to see them as contributing to the larger community, or to recognize their critical historical significance.[2]

Feminists have strongly rejected patriarchy's right to interpret human experience and to determine what the gospel means. As women have become aware that their well-being and their religious experiences have been ignored, trivialized, or denied, they have developed a "suspicion" about all externally given interpretations of the meaning of Christianity for them.

For women who identify themselves as feminists and Christians and who choose to work within church and seminary structures, an understanding of their own authority and the authority they give to others is critical. It determines the way they address the following questions. What do they find as trustworthy in their search for religious meaning? What and whom do they pay attention to as authoritative for their lives and work? When confronted by the principalities and powers of this world, what do they turn to as the touchstone for their sense of reality? What gives them courage for acting on their convictions? When they are confronted by the principalities and powers that are pervasive in Christian institutions and traditions as well as in the culture in general, what is the basis for their sense of authority? What do they affirm, what do they challenge, what are they willing to risk, and what do they proclaim as good news (gospel)? And finally, how does their understanding of external authority influence the ways they express their own authority personally and through their positions of leadership?

Feminists who confront these serious and basic questions do not claim to have solved them. But they do have some important concerns and critical insights. As women—and members of any group—struggle for liberation, the issue of authority is central. They are challenging entrenched authorities who claim to have tradition, institutions, and reason on their side. These women are keenly aware that many authority issues mask power realities. At the same time that they are confronting "authorities," they are striving to develop authority for their own convictions and work that is not authoritarian or dominating, but empowering and relational. The following material recounts what feminist clergy and theologians have come to understand about their own authority for ministry.

Authority, power, and empowerment

In interviews and conversations with clergywomen, I found that the word "authority" itself evoked very ambivalent responses. Most of these women equate authority with their experiences of church hierarchies, with those who have used the "authority" of the Bible and church history to demonstrate why women should not be ordained, and with male-defined theology. For them it is crucial to acknowledge that the language of authority is often used to disguise the misuse of power. "Our generation of women has learned first of all the importance of power and, second, how men have used the lan-

guage of authority to define religion for women,"
said one woman I interviewed.

Rhetoric about community and servanthood often
obscures these power struggles. A clergywoman listening to these familiar phrases, without previous
experience, may find herself used or taken advan-
tage of. Several women recounted instances when
they were encouraged by those in their church hierarchy to reveal their own vulnerability and real feelings over some incident in order to be collegial.
Later, the women clergy discovered that vulnerability was seen as weakness, and they were then characterized as too emotional or too angry to be treated as
real colleagues. What they had assumed to be an
exchange of honest feelings was, instead, used by
those in power to discredit them. Furthermore, real
conflict and difference have been "resolved" too
often by the use of power, rather than through pro-
cesses of actual encounter and respect.

Experiences such as these make women assess first
of all the power dynamics of the church and society.
They must struggle, realistically, to protect themselves against the misuse of power disguised as
authority. Thus one woman said, "When I enter a
situation where a person or group has the power, I
consider that to be a *negotiation* situation and therefore a situation which calls for thoughtful and sensitive strategizing. *I do not share the vulnerability or
pain of my existence in that situation, but the dignity of my purpose.*"

Another woman said she experienced her relationship with her church hierarchy not as an authority
relationship but as a power struggle. "It is not the
authority of my experience that they listen to, but
my ability to mobilize power." She does not count
upon a process of mutual, respectful exchange about
differences. What she has discovered is that what
others might see as a conflict with authority is often
a confrontation with power. Thus she recognizes that

what the hierarchy might designate as her "authority problem" is really an issue of power. So she works to develop her own empowerment by enlisting supporters, using several strategies to raise issues, and at times being confrontive so that she cannot be ignored because of her lack of institutional power.

A major issue for such women is therefore to be clear about *who has power* and *who needs empowerment.* "It is not that power itself is evil," says one. What is evil is "power *over,* not shared power. It's pretty painful *not* to have power. Look at the faces of battered women, the poor, refugees, minorities—there is pain because of their lack of power. It is shared power I seek." This understanding of power—rejecting dominating power and affirming shared power—is essential for analyzing the meaning of any established authority.

For these women, addressing the power arrangements in their communities is a prerequisite also for understanding their own authority. "I think about power issues every day because it is a dynamic in the lives of all the people in my church. For most of them it is a matter of finding ways to empower their own sense of being alive," said one clergywoman in a small church in a company-run town. The people in her town need to question the established authorities in many areas of existence. They have very little sense of their own power in determining the shape of their lives. The meaning of religious experience has often been defined for them by clergy. In this situation she does not want to become another authority figure. She sees her role as encouraging the people to develop their own sense of authority about their faith experiences and their own power in shaping their lives in the community.

Another clergywoman in a wealthy and highly professional congregation saw herself as having very limited power. Most decisions about congregational life were in the hands of a few men who were also

powerful in the larger community. She used her status as a clergyperson to resist the domination of these
men. Thus, she wielded the power of her office to
confront the men's use of their power. She recounted
how she felt a sense of achievement when she
learned how to organize meetings so that others who
were present—and not only the few men—were able
to make important decisions for the church.

Both these women were struggling with how to
understand authority through first grappling with issues of power. They were and are trying to establish
an authority that comes from their own empowerment rather than from power *over.* They are learning to use their own power to help others claim the
power of their own lives, and they struggle against
those who try to claim power over them. Feminists
address authority for ministry by examining first how
any authority of role, person, scripture, or history is
actually functioning. To clarify authority issues they
ask whether claims to authority mask power over
them, or whether the authority is an empowering
agency. For instance, even when scripture is seen to
empower women, the way it functions within a specific context determines its actual meaning in people's lives. Many women who have read the story of
Mary and Martha in the Bible have encountered a
sense of liberation, of empowerment. This story has
been seen as an example of Jesus affirming a woman
who refuses to be in the kitchen while the men dis-
cuss affairs of state. On the other hand, the story is
incomplete because it does not address the empowerment of Martha. The Marthas of this world need to
be heard from before we can assume that this story
is authoritative for women. There is another story
that needs to be told from Martha's experience of
what liberates her when food must be cooked and
people fed. It is not just a matter of interpretation. It
is a matter of what actually empowers. If this story is

to function as an authority for women, it still needs to hear from Martha.

Authority, experiential and relational

Feminists claim that authority for ministry must be situated in honest and reflective discourse of women about their *own* experiences-in-relationship. The realities of a sexist world and a patriarchal religion require that women start from reflection upon personal experience.

Thus, authority for the claims of the Christian faith begins with women's reflection upon their own experiences as interpreted within their own particular historical and social context. They start with reflection upon their own feelings, stories, and encounters with God and others. According to Ruether, the question of principle to be addressed to a biblical interpretation, history, creed, or institution is whether it "denies, diminishes, or distorts the full humanity of women." If it does, it is not redemptive.[3] As Ruether elaborates, feminist theology draws on women's experience as "the basic source of content as well as a criterion of truth," not because "experience" is the unique feminist method of interpretation but because all theologies start from particular human experiences. What is unique to feminist theology is that it is reflection upon *women's* experience.[4]

The women clergy, like the feminist theologians, find their sense of authority rooted in their experience. Experience is tested, examined, and made meaningful within one's use of reason, tradition, and other people's experiences, but the starting point is honoring the validity of one's own experience. These women clergy are very articulate about valuing their own religious experiences.

Furthermore, we know what we know through our

experiences as bodies-in-relationship. To claim that all experience is embodied, says Beverly Wildung Harrison, is to understand that *"perception* is foundational to *conception.* Ideas are dependent on our sensuality. Feeling is the basic bodily ingredient that mediates our connectedness to the world."[5] The traditional Christian split between body and soul, nature and spirit, bodily desires and agape love has served to disconnect us from the root of our knowledge—our bodies. Feminists have documented how this dualistic approach to body and spirit has augmented negative views of women's ability to be "spiritual" leaders. Says Harrison: "When we cannot feel, literally, we lose our connection to the world. All power, including intellectual power, is rooted in feeling. If feeling is damaged or cut off, our power to image the world and act into it is destroyed and our rationality is impaired. But it is not merely the power to conceive the world that is lost. Our power to value the world gives way as well."[6] Of course, we need to reflect upon and decide what to do with what we experience. But the religious meaning of our experiences comes from our ability to be "in touch" with our deepest bodily feelings in order to connect with God and others.

One important way to recapture the connection of embodied experience is to pay attention to what is often referred to as "intuition." For many clergy-women, claiming personal authority requires that they start to trust and explore their "intuitions"— that sense of bodily unease that occurs when one "feels" something is not quite right. Often, women are counseled to ignore such feelings if they cannot immediately connect them with the apparent framework of knowledge that is operating. However, women have discovered that if they begin to pay attention to these signals of the body-self and give them validity and reflect upon them, they often uncover critical insights into what is really going on. It is a signal from the body to begin questioning what is happening. Intuition in this sense is not anti-intellectual feeling as contrasted with thought. It can be a perception or reaction to a situation or condition which signals that something is wrong; that something in the context may be distorted or ignored.

If respected and analyzed, intuition can lead to valuable insight. For women in a sexist culture, paying attention to intuition can be an important clue to the need to examine what is happening. One woman who attends frequent meetings with church officials and colleagues sums up what many women do in using intuition to find a clue to explore and analyze. "I have learned over time to pay close attention to my instinct in those meetings. I used to dismiss my feelings of unease because I did not have immediate verbal responses, but I've discovered that I need to pay attention to my instinct—something is usually going on that is not being acknowledged." Another woman initially expected to rely heavily on her academic and intellectual resources for her ministry. But she discovered that it was her intuition which provided the first clues to confusing situations. "I have had my feelings deeply confirmed," she said. "When I take time to analyze those feelings, I find important insights for my work." Thus, women pay attention to intuition because it is a signal: something needs to be examined, and assumptions need to be questioned. Paying attention to their feelings as a clue to what becomes personally authoritative is one way these women learn to respect the validity of their own experiences and develop a sense of personal authority.

This understanding of the experiential base for personal authority relates directly to women's role as clergy. Their authority for their beliefs comes from their faith *experience.* Thus, women clergy have learned that to speak authoritatively about faith is essentially to speak experientially about faith. "No

creed or structure can be substituted for the authority of my own experience," said one woman. This
learning comes both from feminism and from the
local parish. "When I started my ministry, I didn't
know that, but the people in the church taught me
that the real affirmation of faith comes through faith
experience."

Said another, "One of the most difficult parts of
being a pastor and preacher is the inherent need to
be transparent, to allow others to see into myself, to
lay bare my soul. And what do I mean exactly? It
seems that *appropriate* honesty about one's faith and
life experience is necessary in order to convey the
Word in a compelling and credible manner. I connect my own hurts, questions, and experiences to
what the faith is about and enter with others into the
search for truth and meaning."

In telling their own stories of faith, these women
clergy encourage people of the parish to share their
own struggles and experiences of faith. By speaking
out about their own experiences, they encourage
others to speak honestly about their faith experiences as well. As one woman said, "What I learned in
the parish was that people wanted value and meaning in the experiences of their *own* lives. To show
that it was meaningful for people in the Bible or in
different times is not adequate to what they need. It
is always a matter for this time, these circumstances,
this place, these people."

Another important and critical aspect of experience is its relationality. To claim the authority of
one's own experience is not to be individualistic. The
self is formed in the interweaving of relationships.
We are formed within a network, not as autonomous
beings but as individuals whose very sense of self is
informed and shaped in relationship to others, our
earth, and our experiences of God. Each person is
both unique and part of a larger interwoven reality.
Each person has something to offer to the total reli-

gious experience. At the same time, we cannot totally understand ourselves, let alone others, until we
can understand the relationships that are always in-
forming and shaping the connections. To comprehend our own experiences more fully requires that
we validate our unique constellation of relationships
as we learn how the experiences of others illuminate
the relational basis of our personhood. Again, as Harrison explains, "Nothing living is self-contained; if
there were such a thing as an unrelated individual,
none of us would know it."[7]

"My experiences are always experiences of relationship and community," was reported over and
over by women clergy whom I interviewed. Their
sense of authority is shaped by their understanding
of their experience as participants in the historic
faith and in their particular commitments-in-com-
munity. Therefore, their sense of the authority of
their work in a particular setting comes from being
part of a community that can share experiences of
concerns, visions, covenants, and activities together.
This affects both their role in a community and their
confidence in their beliefs and concerns. "I became
pastor not when I was appointed but when the community actually experienced me as pastor," said one.
"To speak with authority comes when one speaks out
of and to the collective experience."

The authority for their own work is enhanced not
in denying a particular faith experience, or elevating
another, but in sharing experiences in community in
the hope that the possibility of a common faith and
a relational sense of authority will emerge.

Therefore, it is important to women clergy to work
to create the conditions in which faith experiences of
many people can be mutually and justly shared. This
is an exciting and potentially important aspect of
these feminist ministers' struggles with authority.
Outside of the churches in which testimonies are
publicly expected, Protestants in the United States

today rarely share with each other the events and experiences of their lives that have formed their deepest beliefs. In many mainline Protestant congregations, people may worship on Sunday for decades without having the faintest idea about the deepest convictions of the believer next to them. This is sad and destructive for the creation of community and for our understanding of the formation power of our relationships.

Indeed, these women report that they spend much effort in encouraging members of the congregation to respect and to listen to this sharing of faith experiences. Conditions of trust-building and of good listening need to be put in place so that people who share their deep vulnerabilities and convictions are not wounded or held in contempt. This is extremely important. Often those who have been through the theological education system seem to have a veiled sense of contempt for the piety of the believers in their pews. They may resist lay preaching because the laity do not understand exegesis or have "bad theology." For these feminists, however, it is very important to begin from a strong sense of respect and honor for the faith experiences of all believers. It is also important to ensure that conditions exist that make such respect and honor more likely to prevail—conditions of mutuality and equality. Then we can learn to be truthful about our faith experiences and not fear differences.

Hierarchical church systems that do not provide this mutuality and equality can neither claim a woman's trust nor be authoritative for her. These women find that their own authority as clergy comes when they claim the power of their own experiences and expect others to claim the same power. Then, in mutual exchange, a faith relationship can develop. That relationship—not their ordination or their role—forms the basis of their authority for ministry. They are not naive about the power dynamics of their clergy role. But they want to be clear that they understand their authority for their witness as coming from their faith experience, not from the role.

This means that the authority of experience requires that people speak as honestly as they can about commitments and doubts. To speak truthfully about one's experience is the basis for personal authority. To act authoritatively we must try to tell the truth about our life of faith: what really motivates us, what we really value, what has given us sustenance and courage, what names we choose in order to express faith experience, to whom we are loyal.

Only in telling the truth of our experiences do we create the possibility for trust and more truth-telling to develop around us. When people find we tell the truth about ourselves, we help create the conditions of trust. Trust allows us to be open to the truth of others' experiences and thus be open to others' insights, knowledge, and meaning. For many of the women clergy, the poet Adrienne Rich has articulated this need most powerfully:

> Truthfulness anywhere means a heightened complexity. But it is a movement into evolution. Women are only beginning to uncover our own truths; many of us would be grateful for some rest in that struggle; would be glad just to lie down with the shreds we have painfully unearthed and be satisfied with those. . . . [However,] the politics worth having, the relationships worth having, demand that we delve still deeper.[8]

The faith we hold, the new creation we are building, demands the "complexity" of our truths.

If we do not have to fear power over us or the misuse of our own power, we can transform our experience-sharing. When we do not need to fear the denial of our own experiences of the meaning of our lives, we can risk vulnerability and new ways of being together that might enhance our common welfare. We can acknowledge other experiences, not only when they affirm our own but also when they challenge us. At these points, other experiences can become authoritative if we encounter them in mutuality and shared power. Then they may also lead to transformation.

The authority of women's religious experience resides, then, in the honesty we bring to the recounting of our feelings, our story-telling, and our encounters with the holy, and in our relationships to other humans and all of creation. It requires a valuing of and deep respect for the integrity of each unique person and a willingness to be open and vulnerable to one another's feelings and stories. It is in this way that we can hope not only to claim the religious significance of women's experience as authoritative but also to work toward the possibility that we will understand more fully our connections to others. If we meet in mutuality we may find common bonds of authority for our lives together.

Thus, to speak out of the authority residing in women's experience is not to deny the place of reason, tradition, or scripture. Rather, it is to know that these "authorities" are always mediated through specific contexts and particular people's experiences. It is to claim the necessity of reflecting upon our own experiences and also to recognize the limitations of any group making claims for others about what is *the* truth, *the* tradition, or *the* meaning of life and the holy. As women who are confronting the power of a patriarchal tradition, we claim that the foundation of our authority must reside in women's experiences of the holy and women's insights into what contributes to women's well-being as part of God's creation. There is no other starting place.

Co-authoring the tradition

As women tell the stories of their own faith experiences and reflect upon them, they discover that the tradition of Christian faith is not just something that comes to them from elsewhere. Rather, they are themselves transforming and changing the tradition of faith under new conditions. Like the saints before them, they are "authors" and originators of the faith—and in this sense they find a source of authority in actually contributing to the stories of the tradition.

Because they have stories to tell and names to give of their experiences of God and of the meaning of life, they actually become authors. They contribute actively to the tradition through the *addition* of their stories, as well as through their interpretation of earlier portions of the tradition. The meaning of Christianity was not established once and for all. It is always being revealed in particular contexts. Thus the issue is not to establish once and for all what is the tradition or to decide who Jesus was but, according to Ruether, to continue to explore what to do with our lives in the context of our own experiences of the biblical stories, our own participation in slavery, exodus, wandering, and glimpses of a promised land. Letty Russell adds that each community has the responsibility to "show and tell" what God has done in their lives.[9] To claim co-authorship of the tradition is to assert that we have equality of authority with all others to participate with God in the development of the community of faith.

Acting as co-creators of God's promise of love and justice

The authority for our ministry also comes as we take on the responsibility for living out the implications of the gospel for our lives. As women claim the power to name their experiences of life's meaning, they then have the responsibility to work out the implications of their faith commitments. With the recognition that each person should have the power to interpret and create meaningful life comes the ethical need to be a responsible and faithful witness. Christian faith becomes authoritative for women not only as they participate in the development of the tradition but as they engage in the act of *co-creating* the Christian vision for the future. Human beings take on authority as they participate in the ethical act of creating new possibilities for life. They do this through claiming power to name and to act toward the future.

Feminists understand human activity as social and interdependent activity. What we know of human goodness and human sin is that it is incorporated in human activity over time—through history. At the same time, feminists honor the possibility for individuals to act with freedom and thus act responsibly. Human freedom is also possible. As we understand the dynamics of good and evil, we make choices about how we live out moral options and how we see new possibilities for our future. These choices in freedom are not abstractions. Tragically, oppression in history means we do not all have equal access to participating with power in creating new possibilities for human life. People's potential for shaping those possibilities, according to Ruether, is related to their consciousness of their capacity to name their own experiences, in envisioning new ways of being together, and in their access to the resources of social, political, cultural, and religious power. But we must act with the freedom we do have, even though it is limited.

Systems of exploitation and oppression have, in particular, suppressed the equal participation of women. Yet we do not face a predetermined future. "More of the same" is not the Christian hope. The past does not define the future as long as we understand that the past was not inevitable; it was the result of particular visions, actions, and power arrangements. That past suppressed the equal participation of women; therefore we have not yet seen what might be possible as we claim responsibility as co-creators of new visions and new relationships.

We are co-creators with others and God. This means, says Letty Russell, that we are called to work out of an anticipation of a new future as the basis of our hope, not out of the limitations of the past. The authority for ministry comes as women claim responsibility for their own lives and contribute to the collective task of envisioning what God's new creation means for the full humanity and well-being of women and of all the world.

To say that we are active agents in the creation of the future does not imply that we will necessarily choose a future of liberation, *shalom,* and love. We may choose destruction. Even more demonically, a few may have enormous power to effect that destruction. To say that we have the potential for creating is not to claim that we will become more enlightened and that progress is inevitable; rather, it is to claim that we do make choices for good or evil and that those choices *do* make a difference. What we need to understand is that as co-creators we are involved in social and political creation. That means we need to understand the connections between our personal lives and public issues, so that we can understand more fully how our activity is in fact related to our vision and how we are acting responsibly with the freedom we do have and thus with the authority of co-creators.

Resources that inform authority for ministry

Reflection upon the meaning of experience does not occur in a vacuum. For the women clergy I interviewed there were critical dialogue partners within and without the Christian communities and some very important resources for their own sense of authority.

Bible

Responses to the Bible provide possibly the widest range of opinions. For some, the Bible has been a continuous source of empowerment. For these women, the paternalism of the biblical tradition and its cultural limitations are offset by its message of liberation and by their perception of the activity of Jesus and his "counter-culture" relations to women. The Bible has been such a positive part of these women's lives that they are more confident in refuting passages and interpretations that devalue women than they are distrustful of its use in disempowering women. For them the Bible is authoritative because it speaks to their experience and is compelling in its message. "When I say that the Bible is my authority, I am also saying that I consider myself one of the biblical people—one of the people involved in creating the message," claims one clergywoman. As coauthors of the tradition, feminist theologians such as Ruether, Harrison, and Russell also continue to find faith companions within the biblical tradition. In particular, they consider the prophetic tradition and Jesus' story-telling to compel their faith journey and provide insight, challenge, and validation of their religious pilgrimages.

Ruether considers the Bible to contain subversive material providing a critical foundation for poor and oppressed peoples.[10] The New Testament parables often subvert the existing order by asking a new question about life situations: "You have heard it said that . . . but I say to you. . . ." Women need to ask their own new questions and give their interpretations as partners in the development of the tradition.

"Jesus," says Harrison, is an "irreplaceable forerunner in the process of redemption, but not as our replacement in that work." Therefore, Jesus was not the end of revelation, but opens the way for our revelations.[11] Thus Jesus is our companion in the faith journey—the one who refused to abandon us even in death.

For other women clergy, the Bible is much more closely affiliated with a tradition that is limited in its direct application and meaning for today's religious issues. For these women the Bible is the stepping-stone for the task of creating their own faith values. None, however, claims that the Bible must be the essential source of authority for all other persons. The claims these women make for its authority reside in their own experience in faith communities.

What all these women advocate in their work is not that one negate one's own experience but rather that one enter into dialogue with the Bible. They welcome Letty Russell's emphasis on the Bible as a partner in the journey of the Christian community. As a partner it has its own integrity; the meaning it holds for people's lives arises from the interchange, not from some external criteria of what is authoritative. Particular communities, bringing the integrity of their experience, find in the dialogue self-revealing insight, support, judgment, and vision. The biblical story is informed by the encounter of particular people with Jesus and his friends. Thus it continues to be newly interpreted as long as Christian communities continue to be living communities.[12] Russell's emphasis on dialoguing with the Bible was echoed by one of the clergywomen:

"I stake my life on the hope and meaning of life that I find in the biblical tradition. However, I certainly do not accept the claims of those passages which place women subordinate to men or which tell slaves to obey their masters; nor do I believe that all people must find the Bible to be the essential resource for the meaning of their lives, *even though it is for me.*"

Experience of suffering

Another important resource for a feminist sense of authority comes from experiences of suffering and participation in the suffering of others. How people face suffering is critical for what they learn about being human. The insights, courage, and strength that people who face the pain of suffering exhibit are compelling as resources for the meaning of life. This resource for authority is particularly vivid to clergy-women as they deal with the sick or dying and as they listen to the experiences of local people. These women clergy do not romanticize suffering, nor do they claim that suffering is good. But they do know that suffering is real. They know that those who face it, who confront evil and mystery and learn how to live through it, can develop wisdom that helps them to endure, continue struggling, and practice hope. It is the stories of people—"the saints," who do not give up, who continue to hope, who do not lie about suffering—that provide a rich resource for the authoritative activity of these women clergy.

Energy of anger

Yet another resource gives these clergywomen courage to act out their commitments and becomes one of the bases of their sense of authority: the energy of their anger at injustice, at violation, and at situations that could be changed. They talked about anger as a resource and as a source of strength. One woman recounted her experience as one group in her church tried to get rid of her. Her anger at the methods and injustice of the situation kept her from succumbing to the pain of rejection and alienation. It gave her the support to maintain her sense of confidence in her experiences and to resist attempts to trivialize her sense of outrage. Another reported that when she got in touch with anger caused by injustice or violation of herself, she found both energy and clarity. She said, "My unexamined feelings of anger can become self-destructive if I lash out at others without consciousness about the source of my anger. Anger that is repressed becomes depression. But when I get in touch with the source of any anger I gain clarity about myself, I find my own authority, and I find energy—passion for acting to stop the injustice or the violation of myself or others."

Spiritual experiences

The women clergy are very careful about articulating the resources of their spiritual experiences and the power they experience in relationship to God. For them, traditional Protestant language about spiritual experience can obscure what they want to express. Language about spirituality can be used to separate mind, body, and spirit or to separate the spiritual from the political. They are very much aware that behind the demand that "the church should deal with the spiritual needs of people and stay out of politics" is the assumption that the spiritual can be disconnected from the political. They reject that assumption. They are also aware that much dialogue about spirituality tends to be personalistic rather than communal. People seldom address the spiritual health of the community as if it were *essential* to the spiritual health of the individual. There is little emphasis on the relationship of individual spiritual development to community spiritual growth, nor is spiritual development necessarily understood as the development of the body politic. These women wish to reject such views but are often at a loss for a language that can truly express what they experience. One woman talked about spirituality as the "shared, and hopefully ever deepening, passion of the community." They also find that language about spirituality has been used to quantify experience. Some people are thereby described as more spiritual than others, as though one person's life experiences can be judged as of higher quality than another's. One woman said that she does not talk about the deep mystical experiences she has had. When she tries to communicate them, she is seen as either weird or more holy, depending on the context. The tendency of others to see her mystical experience as "special revelation" makes her wary of exposing it. She is careful, therefore, never to claim that the Holy Spirit is the source of her authority, even when the image of the Holy Spirit seems appropriate for expressing her experience.

"I don't deny the power of the Holy Spirit, but I don't claim it as the source of my authority, because that perpetuates what has been done to me—others claiming external sources for their actions against me. I prefer to claim responsibility for my own actions, while not denying the power of the holy in my life."

Yet the power of the holy, the power of prayer-filled lives, the power of meditation, and the imagery that comes are for these women very important resources for claiming the authority of their own faith experience. As one said, "Even the patriarchal tradition has been unable to control spirituality. The church may have its doctrines, its offices, its theology, but it has never been able to control the passion that is evoked by women's experiences of the holy in their lives."

Through all these encounters with others, and with traditions and scriptures, these women clergy find resources for their own sense of authority ("confidence" is the word one woman preferred) in their respect for the wholeness of life and in the struggle to live out a life of faithfulness in particular communities. "It may sound simplistic," said one woman, "but trying to live truthful and faithful lives—not perfect, but with a willingness to try—is the most powerful authority that one has."

Authority and the example of preaching

One of the areas of ministry where authority issues are raised is the act of preaching. The Protestant denominations to which these women belong consider preaching to be a major function of the clergy. The clergyperson is often called the "preacher." The most visible sign of a pastor's work is the Sunday morning sermon. Church people have expressed doubts about whether women can preach "with authority." The skill and "authority" with which one preaches often determine the "box office" attraction of a church. In my talks with women clergy, preaching was an area in which authority issues were frequently raised.

Preaching, for these women, occurs in the context of the larger setting of worship. Worship is not seen as primarily a setting for the sermon, because worship is the activity of the whole gathered community. Those who have been in local congregations for longer periods have developed more congregational involvement in every aspect of worship. But all are committed to the community's claiming its own worship life, including its preaching.

They make it clear to their congregations that their own experience is the basis for their insight in preaching. This is critical for two reasons. First, they want to respect diversity of experience. "I preach out of my own experience," said one woman. "That is what I claim, and thus I say to the people in the congregation, 'That is what I expect from you; not conformity to my ideas but honest reflection upon your own experience.'"

Second, it is important to these women to preach

experientially to tell people that the source of authority is embodied in one's life. "When I first came, the complaints about my sermons were that they were too emotional and personal. But," says this woman, "I continued to preach that way until the people in my congregation began to see that what I was doing was affirming their right to reflect seriously upon their own faith experiences." Since that time, people in her congregation have begun to reflect upon and share their faith. About twenty people in the congregation have preached. The experience is empowering. Hearing their friends reflect upon their own faith and its meaning for them, people know that it is possible for them also to share their own faith, to challenge each other, and to change. Their own faith is not dead, inaccessible, private, or irrelevant. For this pastor, the growth in the number of "preachers" in the congregation is a sign of the authority of her own preaching.

Another woman puts her sermon together through the process of weekly visits with people in her church and through sharing experiences, feelings, and concerns. The authenticity of her preaching depends upon the connections she can make between her experiences and those of people in the church. She says, "Even when I preach on very controversial issues, I start, not with my conclusions, but with the concerns and questions of people in the community. Even when I'm very clear about my own stand, my function in the pulpit is not as authority figure but as one willing to enter into the struggle for common vision."

While recognizing that they are not unique in their understanding of preaching, these women clergy feel nevertheless that preaching has too often been an announcement about the Word or is seen as the particular work of the pastor. Because they believe that authority for any community needs to come out of careful reflection upon *everyone's* faith experiences, they strive to make worship, including the sermon, the work of the whole people. Thus they are experimenting with a variety of ways that the whole congregation can participate in the preaching act. These feminists' approach to preaching illustrates how they understand their own personal authority and how they act out their authority as clergy.

Conclusion

The truth of the Christian faith for these feminists, both theologians and clergy, is rooted in their own relational faith experiences. The Christian faith cannot be authoritative just on the basis of particular creeds, historical interpretations, biblical exegesis, or the insights of human sciences. The authority of the Christian faith is finally dependent upon its actual transforming activity in life experiences. By viewing authority in this way, women can encounter the experiences of the Christian community through the ages without having to deny the validity of their own experience or acquiesce in their own subjugation.

These women speak out of the authority of particular experiences. They are careful not to assume a universal authority. They cannot speak for all until all people have an equal opportunity to speak about their search for meaning and value in their lives. Knowing what it means to have their own faith experiences denied or distorted, these women theologians and clergy are committed to working for the time when all people can express their own faith experiences.

It is very important to see that these claims of authority for ministry are rooted in the embodied experiences of people-in-relationship. To claim that the Christian faith is authoritative is not only to find resource, insight, and affirmation for the meaning of one's life experiences within its traditions and communities but also to contribute to the story itself. The

process of claiming this authority involves co-author-
ing the faith. The authority of the Christian faith does
not reside in its claim to uniqueness or in a specific
revelation, but in its power to speak to women's experiences of life's value and meaning, in its power to
include their experiences and to move them to act as
witnesses to its truth in their lives.

These feminists, both theologians and clergy, claim
that their authority is rooted in their own experience
and has integrity and significant meaning. It is an
authority that also has limits. These women do not
claim to speak for everyone. They believe it is important not to overgeneralize about *the* human condition, nor to assume that the experiences and insights
of women can hold for everyone. That is what was
done to them and they are wary of doing it to others,
especially others of marginalized groups. They want
to model not only how authority for ministry is
claimed but also how authorities are critiqued. Faith
is revealed through the particular experiences of
people and groups. The authority for universal faith
assertions cannot be made then until all persons and
groups have the freedom to express their faith experiences. Only in the mutual sharing of faith experiences in communities of shared power can the truth
and the meaning of lives be fully expressed and
known. That has not yet happened.

The experiences of each particular group or person have their own integrity and validity. Yet experience is always relational. The women theologians
and clergy agree that authority is rooted in particular
experiences and that those experiences are per-
meated by community meaning and interwoven
with the lives of others. Thus, they say, if we consciously seek to understand the web of relatedness
out of which our particular experiences are formed,
we can begin to discover connections that make
unity and common faith possible.

In claiming the authority of faith, they do not feel

the need to refute other options for faith claims. As Christians, they find meaning in the Christian stories as these become their story. They are called to co-author their tradition and co-create their future. They are called to be faithful to the truth they experience, not to be obedient to external authority or to be authoritarian.

Personal authority is rooted in honest examination of our own experiences of life and sacred meaning. The authority of religious communities arises out of the connections made when people are free to engage in mutual exchange about their most passionate experiences of the holy.

3

Salvation as New Creation

Christians proclaim that Jesus had a message of good news, a message about the meaning of our lives that literally "saves us." For some, salvation has been interpreted to mean that Jesus' actions save us from the power and effects of sin; to others salvation means deliverance from spiritual isolation and estrangement; some see it as redemption from eternal damnation; for others it is liberation from illusions about our power to control life; and still others see it as the offer of God's presence among us as a sign of God's grace-filled action. There are certainly many other interpretations. The concern here is to show that the way we interpret salvation affects how we understand ministry. Thus it is important to look at several themes that emerge from feminist interpretations of salvation. Their reflections on salvation come from the distinctive faith experiences of women as they encounter Christianity.

For feminists, the meaning of salvation is glimpsed in Jesus' explanation to his disciples that they are no longer servants but friends (John 15:15); in the promise that Jesus' friends will do still greater things than he has done (John 14:12); in Jesus' association with the lowly and the outcasts (Luke 7:34); and in the promise of new being and new creation (2 Cor. 5:15). It is an invitation to a new covenant through participation in communities of hope and vision. This new creation invites our active engagement, not in the old sense of works versus faith but in the sense of co-creation, as we saw in the last chapter. This vision of new creation affirms both mutuality of relationship and diversity of insights, gifts, and cultures. We are not to become like each other, but to discover how our differences and our uniqueness enhance life to-gether. New creation is not only glimpsed as a vision that compels our hope, it is also experienced in our daily lives when the love of God is found in and between us. Affirming the broad vision of a trans-formed society is one of the challenges of feminism. It requires a spirituality embodied in encounters of ever more deepening love. This is a spirituality that is rooted in our sexuality—in our ability to touch, feel, bond, and experience intimacy—in our ability to love ourselves, God, and others. This spirituality is the connection between the vision and the everyday reality of people's lives. We need to look at the im-plications of these themes of salvation in more detail.

Utopian vision: Without vision the people perish

Feminists are visionaries. They are engaged in the creation of utopias. They envision social structures that have not yet been realized and they believe in possibilities for human relationships that have not yet been actualized. Thus, they challenge the as-sumptions of defenders of the present "reality" who assume that what may be unrealizable in our *given* order of life is unrealizable in *any* order. Feminists believe that humanity is not limited by the past as long as we can envision something different. They believe this though they know, as Beverly Wildung Harrison says, that "the visionary element is, as yet, quite literally *no where.*"[1] They also claim that it is not "other-worldly." As they envision the new crea-tion, they are also naming the conditions that would make the vision realizable in the present. The vision gives direction for present struggles. It also suggests concrete strategies for breaking down old orders and building a new one. Being able to envision new possibilities for life gives us clues for new ways of acting now.

The past history of Christianity and the past experiences of women can be a resource for the future, but all past models are subject to critique. If we just depend upon the "evidence" of history, women will be caught in the socialization of past values. Women can draw upon the past, but they also need to image new ways of being that are "not yet."

As Christians, these women experience Jesus as one who also laid claim to a vision for a new humanity that has the possibility of going ahead to an as yet unrealized future, specifically a different order of things where the last are first and the least are honored—an order he called the "Kingdom of God."

Ruether states that this new order is not just a social form but a new "social vision, a new soul . . . , a new type of social personality" that we might even call a "new religion" if we take prophetic vision seriously.[2] Russell talks about this perspective as "advent shock," maladjustment with the present because of a longed-for future. Instead of looking only to the past or the original church or the actual words of Jesus, we look for the promises of God breaking into the present as a pull toward the future.[3]

Feminist visions of the promise of new creation include a world where nobodies are somebodies, where women and men experience mutuality, and where justice is the norm of life. God's intention for us is love and mercy in a relationship of solidarity. God is envisioned as advocate, as the spirit of empowerment, as our companion who challenges and supports, as one who is always with us through suffering and joy. The more that feminists can fill out these visions, the more help we will have in knowing how to act our way into the future we envision. The salvation story is the good news that we are not trapped by the past but are freed to envision a future that sustains what we long for. Furthermore, the process of envisioning that future provides us with clues for our present life. We can become what we can envision. The realm of God is not an illusion.

This understanding of salvation asserts that human freedom is possible. We can reconstruct present personal, social, political, and economic realities. This freedom is not some quality we possess as an absolute. We know that the freedom to create a new life is conditioned on the actions of others. It is, however, says Russell, the belief that if we continue to envision a new creation, we will have a source of hope and a way of acting *now* that keeps the possibility of freedom open.[4]

Those who can believe in the possibility of a new creation can also live as if that promise is already present. They expect that each day provides new opportunities to learn what it means to live into the vision. Thus conversion is understood as the ongoing experience of practicing the vision in ever-expanding ways. We expect that as we practice living out the vision, it will be revealed more fully.

Affirmation of difference and of community

One of the most powerful elements of the vision of new creation is the experience of communities in which difference is not feared, but actually enhances the common life. The poet Audre Lorde expresses the sense of what this hope can mean when she says:

> Difference must be not merely tolerated, but seen as a fund of necessary polarities between which our creativity can spark like a dialectic.

Only then does the necessity for interdependency become unthreatening. Only within that interdependency of different strengths, acknowledged and equal, can the power to seek new ways of being in the world generate, as well as the courage and sustenance to act where there are no charters. . . .

As women, we have been taught either to ignore our differences, or to view them as causes for separation and suspicion rather than forces for change. Without community there is no liberation, only the most vulnerable and temporary armistice between an individual and her oppression. But community must not mean a shedding of our differences, nor the pathetic pretense that these differences do not exist.[5]

Groups have often used definitions of salvation to exclude those who are different, classifying as unsaved those who do not exhibit similar cultures, creeds, or common experiences. Over the ages, churches have struggled to determine the true church, the elect. Feminists are particularly sensitive to this history of exclusion of the "different." For them the gospel message, and God's vision for humanity and all creation, is not only that the different are accepted but that their differences provide crucial insight into the salvation story and into the possibility of new creation itself.

For the clergywomen I interviewed, the issue of affirming difference and the attempt to develop community became the same struggle. Said one, "When I came to this church it was directionless. As we worked together I saw that we needed two priorities—acceptance of difference and deeper intimacy. Now whatever we do is conditioned by our vision of inclusion and intimacy. Both priorities help us attend to the need to deepen relationships and to continually expand the boundaries of our collective life. In this way we keep before us the vision of inclusiveness that honors diversity."

Another clergywoman related her work in ministry to her own struggle to be ordained. "I'm not here," she said, "to be absorbed into the system, nor to look like every other minister. That was what the church tried to do when I was ordained, however. It tried to make me like them." Said another, "To honor difference is to make sure that there are no second-class citizens in the church. The homogeneous church is not the church I want to belong to." The women also recognize that to attempt to honor difference and encourage diversity is to challenge major theories of community and to risk the pain of exposing differences in a world where power is not equally shared. One reports that "people tend to want to tell others what they should do and be. Therefore, I know that when I encourage people to become open and vulnerable with who they are, they can also be hurt. To be different and to accept difference is often scary, but for me, it is clearly an issue of justice." As one woman put it, paraphrasing Matthew 5, "What does it profit you to love your own kind? Even the evil ones do that; it is in loving the ones who are different that we discover the *power* of God's love."

To affirm that diversity is good means also to recognize that what we need to do to grow spiritually will mean different things for different people and groups. In learning what it means to share in a community of difference, people will have different things to affirm and will struggle with different issues.

Said one clergywoman, "Doing what is necessary in order to enjoy the gifts of life (salvation) may mean, for some, learning to let go of their desire for material wealth; for others it may mean asserting their right to a share of the material resources. For some it may mean stepping back from positions of authority and power; for others it is the struggle to take on roles of leadership and assume power."

The creation of communities that develop an interdependency that allows differences to spark creativity and new vision and that fosters sharing of power is an awesome task. Yet for these women it is the vision that calls forth their most passionate commitments. For it is in this risk of openness to difference and possible interdependence that salvation is experienced. They do not expect that such community will come about soon. A woman working for ten years in one church expressed her hope by saying that she was deeply thankful when she saw glimpses of community life where "people can live through their crises and not come out destroyed." When that could happen, she experienced a bit of the salvation story.

It is through creating and re-creating bonds of relationship across differences that hope is sustained and the struggle for new life can continue. "We know," said one woman, "that our human existence consists of relationship; none of us is independent, but we live in a matrix of relationships that inform our morality, our sense of purpose, and who we are, and it is these relationships that either expand or diminish life." One clergywoman, when asked about the relation of grace to this struggle for community, said she had found that the two were inextricably bound together. "We have experienced sources of energy to live in new ways, as well as healing and moments of unmerited grace. Sometimes these experiences of new creation in community seem to come as a gift, sometimes we struggle like crazy to get them." The issue is not between choosing to participate in the salvation story or being given the gift of salvation. To be saved means that people experience moments of grace-filled freedom to express their unique value and creativity *and* engage in chosen loving deeds.

The importance of people being affirmed for their

creativity will be explored more in chapter 5. The issue of experiencing love needs to be addressed more fully now.

Universality of God's love

The emphasis on the affirmation of God's love as God's saving activity available to everyone was especially important to the clergywomen I interviewed. A great number of these women quoted Paul's words in Romans as capturing the grounding of their faith.

> There is nothing in death or life, in the realm of spirits or superhuman powers, in the world as it is or the world as it shall be, in the forces of the universe, in heights or depths—nothing in all creation that can separate us from the love of God [as known] in Christ Jesus. (Romans 8:38–39, NEB)

They feel that although the word "love" is often trivialized, spiritualized, or sentimentalized, the experience of love is still the most powerful message of salvation that the church can give. The church is still one of the few places in our society where people expect to receive some support and care and where they are encouraged to reach out in love and care to others.

This kind of love, which is not bound by convention or dogma or social caste or one's winsomeness or past deeds, is indeed hard to comprehend.

One clergywoman recounted that she had recently been with some friends who made disparaging remarks about clergy who were always saying "God loves you." She immediately disagreed.

"I remember the days in seminary when I also put down people who talked like that, but one of the things I discovered as a parish pastor is that people in this place, at least, have very little sense of that. They need to hear and experience continually that

God does love them and to know how it feels to be loved."

Another woman recounted her anger at finding that most people in her parish had never experienced a loving, present God through their church, because God was usually portrayed as remote and other, as judge and ruling father. She expressed her deep concern over the fact that many did not connect God's love with the power generated by concrete loving relationships. This was vividly portrayed to her when a woman who was a long-term member of the church and had been hospitalized with cancer said to her very simply, "I never knew how to reach God or feel God's love until you explained that we are each some part of God's love."

The love of God cannot be contained within any boundaries or religious categories if we refuse to limit its expression in our lives. For these feminists, salvation is the experience that God's love is with us and we can extend it in life or death, beyond all powers and to all people. If we make it concrete, we point to its reality and find that it increases. Love needs expression in order not to be a lie, and yet love is never limited to our expression, but expands with greater power than our cynical times comprehend. That is the good news of the gospel.

The tradition's use of male imagery for God and its tendency to limit God's love to the "saved" have contributed to people's alienation. The belief in the universality of God's love means that none of our limited visions or church structures or creeds can encompass God. Language that limits God to Father has distorted the community's abilities to see women in God's image. Language that assumes God favors Caucasians and Western theologians promotes racism and cultural imperialism. Language about God that assumes God only relates to humans, and not to the totality of creation, makes us careless of the life of this earth. The significance of our use of language, imagery, and metaphor becomes evident when we recognize that our naming literally defines our sense of reality. Refusing to make idols of any language about the presence that sustains our very being is necessary if we accept the universality of a loving "God."

At the same time, these women are not sentimental about the experienced sense of love among people. They see people daily who lack a sense of self-worth, empowerment, and love in their relationships. One clergywoman remarked that she often felt that the basic issue for most people who came to see her was their need for love and a home—a place where they belong. Thus, these women insist that we must push on with the analysis of this issue. It is not enough simply to name the universality of God's passionate love for all—or to name the lack of the lived affirmation of this love. We must connect these issues to the systemic and social forces that perpetuate this distortion of creation. This pushes us onward to examine the relationship between spirituality, personal experience, and social relationship.

Spirituality and sexuality

A feminist analysis of the Christian church's attitude toward women concludes that the churches have perpetuated a fear and hatred of women most powerfully expressed in their attitudes toward sexuality. This negative attitude stems from a dualistic view of life and of the sexes. Woman is associated with the body, feelings, and sexuality; man with the mind, spirit, and rationality. In this view, the mind is superior to and should control the body. Spirituality transcends nature and is therefore superior to our bodily (animal) nature. From this conception of life, all people, men and women, have learned anti-woman feelings and attitudes. Woman's nature and sexuality have been deemed a threat to the very essence of religious life. Sex has been characterized as the power that wars with spiritual energy. Women have been characterized as the source of sexual temptations (Eve, whores, and witches) and have had to deny their sexuality in order to be pure and holy (Mary, Virgin, mother).[6] This view of the world has resulted in a distorted view of humanity and nature. It has, according to Ruether, sanctioned the domination of males over females and ruptured the very basis of the interconnectedness of life.

> The psychic organization of consciousness, the dualistic view of the self and the world, the hierarchical concept of society, the relation of humanity and nature, and of God, and creation— all these relationships have been modeled on sexual dualism.[7]

One has only to look at the depth of emotion generated around issues of sex and sexuality (homosexuality, abortion, birth control) to recognize, at the very least, the church's ambiguous feelings about it. Even though most of the liberal churches have affirmed sexuality as a gift of God, it is clear they feel this gift should be limited, controlled, and private. To be truthful and public about one's sexuality is to risk the deep rage of the church. For example, even in churches that do not openly condemn homosexuality, the homosexual Christian is expected to be quiet or to lie about his or her life-style, rather than making sexual preference a public issue.

Feminists oppose this dualistic, dominant/subordinate view of spirit and body. The very basis of our capacity to love self, God, and others is rooted in honoring our sexuality, not in transcending it. "Our capacity for caring, for expressing and receiving deep feeling, for reaching out to others is grounded in and through our bodies or not at all," says Harrison.[8] Feminists seek to demystify "spiritualistic" themes of human nature. The true gifts of God are life itself and the embodied world of flesh and blood. Women have learned that we are "our bodies, ourselves."

Human sexuality is neither necessarily determined by nature nor antithetical to spiritual love, because "the meaning of our sexuality involves the integration of many levels of biological and social determinants."[9] According to Harrison, the issue facing us is "to appropriate a sexual ethics deep enough to clarify the relation between our capacity for interpersonal love and our ability to struggle effectually for social justice in our common life."[10]

The attitudes and social structures of support around sexuality have implications for all aspects of our lives together: economic, political, and social. Thus, as Harrison writes:

> To have a role in the real healing of people today, to contribute to the genuine empowerment of people, to express radical love in a social context of right relationship (justice), the church must continue to walk the long road of transforming its mores of sexuality. Once and for all, the Christian community must overcome its sexphobic fear of eroticism as a foreign and evil power that wars with positive spiritual energy. We Christians must come to recognize that our sexuality is a foundational aspect of our total, integrated bodily well-being. It is the root of our personal integrity and it must be integrated holistically into our lifestyles and value commitments if we are to possess a deep capacity for intimacy, for powerful communication and rich interaction with others.[11]

The male/female, spirit/body duality that is promoted by both church and culture today has resulted in people being unable to experience love as mutuality. We have not recognized that our personal expressions of love are bound up with our political arrangements. Love of another needs to be both passionate and nonexploitative, but in our culture where race, class, and sex are determined by our lack of mutuality and shared power, many of our experiences of love as the source of our life have been distorted. It is essential to feminists to create love relationships of equality and mutuality. Our sense of spirituality needs to be related to a "healing" sexuality in which the embodied expression of relationships is based on mutuality and equality.

Power is a key issue in any ethics of love. Inequality of power in relationships leads to its misuse. To deepen our spiritual sensitivity, we must become more conscious of the power dynamics of all relationships, from the most intimate to the most public. We need to develop greater possibilities for equality and mutuality in all levels of relationships so that the embodied self touches other embodied selves with care and nurturance and not domination and exploitation. The personal is always political because our ability to love and to extend the meaning of love to a common life is based on our ability to move toward relationships of equality, mutuality, and compassion. As Harrison says:

> Our energy—literally, the gift of life—is body-mediated energy. Our sexuality does not detract from, but deepens and shapes, our power of personal being. Our bodies, through our senses, mediate our real, physical connectedness to all things. Our sexuality represents our most intense interaction with the world. Because this is so, it is also a key to the quality and integrity of our overall spirituality.[12]

The spirituality of a community is revealed in the ways we learn to love ourselves and each other. Our love is embodied in our feelings, our touch, our passion, and our care. If spirituality loses touch with its roots in sexuality, it loses power to form and inform our deepest selves. When sexuality is separated from spiritual development, it becomes something we use to manipulate, control, and harm what we profess to love. When spirituality is separated from our sexuality, it loses the power of personal connection and becomes lifeless—it cannot move us to passionate care for this world.

There are special dilemmas and risks for clergy-women in expressing this vision of spirituality rooted in sexuality. After all, isn't it one of the fears of the church that if women in leadership express their sexuality they will inhibit their effectiveness and their ability to be spiritual guides? There is a deafening silence in churches about what it means to live passionately, with our whole selves, in a world where sex is exploited, where love is separated into boxes labeled eros or agape, where we have learned mostly what is dangerous about passion, instead of how to be life-giving with the power of love. That is why, however, this issue of embodied spirituality is critical to a feminist vision.

Salvation and context

The clergywomen expressed their concern that salvation becomes disconnected from people's experiences both when its meaning is not related to specific contexts and when its radical message is muted by individualistic and disembodied interpretations. They understand that since people live in relationship, salvation cannot be individualistic or isolated from context. People experience salvation in particular relationships and in specific economic, political, and cultural contexts. Community does not exist in general, but in the particular. The vision of new creation is experienced as people endeavor to live out relationships of mutual love in specific situations. However, each context will call for different activities. As one clergywoman remarked, the vision includes "the belief that the community will pay attention to all dimensions of their life and that they will learn how to be responsible and accountable to each other. The example of the early church, where they shared all in common, is not a remote ideal but practical advice."

Three examples of community-building in different churches give insight into what salvation means in particular contexts for these feminists. The constituency of all three churches is mainly white, although the working-class church has strong ethnic ties. In each of these churches people experience personal crises. In each, the clergywomen are concerned to develop caring relationships and respect for the life stories of all the members as they struggle for common goals. However, the work of these women in proclaiming good news is different in each place.

The first church is a city church, a small working-class congregation of Protestants in the midst of a predominantly Roman Catholic population. The people have little power over the forces controlling their lives. The city government, the police, the places where the people work, the social service agencies, and the school are all run by persons outside their community and usually outside their influence or knowledge. Yet many of these people also believe in the American myth that success comes through individual initiative and that failure is a sign of personal inadequacy.

In this working-class church, the clergywoman is both their pastor and an outsider. Well educated and of another class, she represents power over them. Even her most progressive ideas for empowerment must be tested against the reality of what actually empowers these people. They are faced with the basic fact that their sense of self-worth and dignity has been manipulated by forces outside their control.

To be a pastoral leader who witnesses to salvation in this situation means to learn to respect these people and their traditions, to which she is an outsider by culture and class. She must listen, wait, and use her own power carefully. To walk into these people's lives as an educated clergywoman, a professional, with progressive ideas about empowerment and liberation means that she must first and foremost recognize the contradiction of the power relationship she is in and, therefore, her need to learn how her power actually functions in that setting. She represents more than her role as a woman: her access to power is different from many in her church.

The second church, also in an urban setting, is composed of members who are not rich but who comprise a highly educated and progressive group. Many come to the church from other parts of the city. They attend because they all share similar interests and concerns about their mission in the city. These people bring commitments, skills, and energy to the task of building community.

In this urban church with its highly committed and articulate congregation, the clergywoman finds that her function in conveying the good news is much more as support staff. She provides the structures of nurture and support that enable the members to sustain their sense of purpose and that help them organize common undertakings. She is not an outsider but one of a community of skilled persons who, as a group, are able to articulate their faith and express their talents. As a member of the community with particular skills, she acts more as resource person than as leader.

The third church is located in a suburb close to a major city. Its members are highly educated; some have powerful jobs, money, and influence. Many see the church as the place to bring personal problems of comfort and intimacy. It provides continuity in a world of constant change, tension, and conflict.

In this wealthy suburban congregation, the task of bringing good news is exemplified in the fact that this woman represents the marginalized persons in society. Her appointment was opposed by several powerful men in the congregation. They resented a woman in the position of pastor. Simply by being a woman in the clergy role, she represents a minority. In her position of leadership, she represents a concrete reversal of power relationships. In her preaching and education tasks, she explains, she attempts to counter "the religious sense that faith is personalistic piety and being 'better than' others." Her challenge is to repoliticize religion. She explicitly relates faith issues to political issues in order to educate her membership about the connections between their personal lives and world events. Her presence forces the church to confront sexism. Just being the woman pastor provides her with the opportunity to proclaim that Christian community means accepting individual differences. By exposing the connections between the personal and the political, she is demonstrating that the expression of God's love for everyone requires empowerment of the marginalized and relinquishment of power over them.

Thus, these three feminists who share common values find that their leadership functions very differently because of their context and their own relative power. In one context the woman sees her leadership as providing service for empowerment of the members, in another the woman serves as support staff to her colleagues, and in the third the woman represents a reversal of roles in the dominant hierarchy of power.

What then of salvation?

Feminists recognize that their experience of salvation as the power to participate in God's creating love raises some further issues. If the vision of a new creation is somehow related to our power to create, we need to face the fearful side of that promise. If we are co-creators, we do have power to make choices that may affect the future. In fact, it would be much easier to deny our creative power, because it means recognizing that we can use that power to destroy as well as to build up creation. Feminists in our culture know that this nation does, indeed, have power to destroy. But they claim that the greater danger we face is the denial of our part in creating God's realm. If we are unwilling to face our gift of making choices and of creating new possibilities for our world, we are also refusing to admit our participation in evil. We can act as if all is in God's hands and refuse to see and act. This is most powerfully expressed by a story that Dorothee Soelle, a German theologian, told about her own experience in Nazi Germany. She was a young child during World War II. As she grew up, she would ask her parents why they had not protested the extermination of the Jews. "We didn't know," they would reply. But as she learned more about what happened, she found evidence that they did know. She could not understand how they could say "We didn't know." Later, she says, she began reading about nuclear power and the buildup of armaments. She discovered that she would forget the "facts"—the statistics about the realities of the destructive power of nations. She realized that she too was developing a defense against "knowing what she knew" so that she too could say "I didn't know."[13] To know the joy of creating—of bringing beauty, justice, and love—is also to know that we have set before us life and death. Jesus asks us to choose life. We are not passive onlookers in this world. We cannot claim not to know. When we choose to recognize our part in creation, we also must face the fears we have of losing whatever we have of position and privilege in the present power arrangements.

Our desire to choose life means that we refuse to

accept the inevitable, the past, our biological nature, our lack of power. It is our power to envision a new creation that moves us beyond present realities. As Dorothy Dinnerstein says in *The Mermaid and the Minotaur:*

> It is senseless . . . to describe our prevailing . . . arrangements as "natural." They are of course a part of nature, but if they should contribute to the extinction of our species, that fact would be a part of nature too. Our impulse to change these arrangements is as natural as they are, and more compatible with our survival on earth.[14]

As Christians, these women experience Jesus as the one who trusted the vision of God's new creation and showed the power of love to overcome death. He did this not by denying the pain and evil in this world but by refusing to let that be the final word. He constantly expanded people's visions. He told a story about a Samaritan and described a whole new way of being neighborly. He refused to be defeated by evil spirits, those in authority, or even his own priests. When people made the old "wisdom" law, he showed a better way of seeing and acting.

The message of salvation is the promise of a new creation that is embodied in communities of people who dare to create new possibilities for living out love of self, neighbor, and God. They tell the story of salvation, not to make others like them but to offer their own experience of new life. They are discovering ways to affirm that our differences contain our gifts to each other and can lead to greater bonding. As they develop trust and shared vision, the "parts of the body" learn to function together to the mutual benefit of all. As they learn to trust in each other's gifts and in each other's truth-telling, they become extensions of each other and share the work. The community becomes a network of comrades who share strengths and uphold each other. They experience real changes in their lives as they act their way into new visions. They live their way into what they are bold enough to image as encompassing what they most deeply value. Without the vision, their activity is a repetition of what has been. Without their activity the vision becomes illusion.

Feminist affirmations of salvation as "embodied" love—for and between ourselves, God, and others— lead to convictions about the mission of the church, to which we turn now.

4

Mission: Justice and Solidarity

As with any vision that calls for radical change, the
utopian vision of new creation is in danger of becoming an ideology of pious platitudes and sentimentality, or of becoming a new system of oppression in-
stituted by the self-righteous. The mainline churches
in the United States sometimes have been guilty of
the former in rhetoric about love, and guilty of the
latter in some missionary endeavors. Therefore, it is
important to understand what feminists mean when
they say that salvation means new creation. Justice
must be the foundation, as a group of feminist educa-
tors (the Mud Flower Collective) state in *God's Fierce
Whimsy:*

> So strongly do we believe that justice is the foun-
> dation of human life well-lived that we under-
> stand the primary theological task and educa-
> tional task of the churches to be the work of
> justice in the world. . . . No [one] is excused from
> an accountability to human well-being. [All] are
> responsible for calling one another to account
> for whatever apathy toward justice may be ap-
> parent among us.[1]

To be in mission means to act as witnesses to new
creation by becoming involved in liberating activity.

To witness means to show what has given us life. As witnesses, feminists are learning how to act in solidarity with those who do not have access to basic sustenance, to loving relationships, to justice and equality. As witnesses, they are not claiming to know what is ultimate truth, nor are they claiming to be the righteous, but they are saying that they are willing to take responsibility as active partners in the work of justice.

To be a witness to the new creation is to participate in its hope by acts of mutuality and justice: giving and receiving food, drink, clothing, shelter, and comfort. It means engaging in liberating activities with the poor, not because the poor are more virtuous but because their bondage is a sign of the denial of God's justice and love. It means that the "option for the poor" must be exercised if mutuality for all is ever to be achieved. To be witnesses to justice and solidarity means to see all of life as interconnected and to see one's actions as coming out of community witness. To participate in liberating actions is to join in liberating movements. "We are joining," says Russell, "God's protest movement."[2]

Let us look more carefully at some of the elements of mission and its implications for feminist ministry. First, feminists have long emphasized the power of naming as an act of liberation—naming questions, idolatries, and commitments. Second, traditional understandings of service present serious difficulties for feminists. Reinterpreting service as empowerment is crucial for mission. Third, the long-range vision of a radically new creation requires us to attend to specific acts of care and hope now in order that we may be sustained over time. Otherwise the challenge of the vision makes us despairing and disempowered. Last, we need to look at some signs of ways to live in solidarity in the local parish.

The power of naming: Questions, idolatries, commitments

Feminists are particularly sensitive to the power of language to inform and shape reality. Therefore, as these women define mission, they ask whether their language—their acts of communication—reinforces injustice or provides insight and images for liberation. As new consciousness emerges, new meanings, new framing of questions, and new imagery must also find expression. Naming becomes an important liberating function for all oppressed and marginalized people. They must undertake, says Russell, the tasks of defining their own experiences, raising their own questions, examining their idolatries, and developing new imagery for their expression of mission.[3]

Naming questions

Two major questions predominate for feminists as they observe a world that is in danger of destroying itself and rife with unequal power relationships. First, they ask whether there is the possibility of a *gracious neighbor.*[4] Given the depth of the oppressive systems that people have participated in and been dominated by, is there any possibility of people finding ways to live together peacefully, justly, and lovingly? A second question for feminists is: Given the fact that their own largely white, Western Christian church has participated in the divisiveness and subjugation of people, does the church in the United States have a mission relevant to a pluralistic world?

A host of other questions follow from these two regarding the power of the church and its relationship to the world. Some of these questions are: Whose values and interests are women theologians serving? What kinds of political commitments must one make in light of continued poverty and oppression

throughout the world? What signs for hope and survival exist in the face of chronic environmental abuse
and nuclear proliferation? Is resisting evil the best
white Americans can do? Or is it possible actively to
contribute to liberation? Can the Christian church
offer justice in its own structures for the half of the
human race that is female? Can Western Christianity
promote a vision of inclusiveness in light of its anti-
Semitism, religious intolerance, and racist and class
structure in the United States? Can the church participate in economic and political justice and resist
compliance with an imperialist, consumer-oriented
economy?[5]

These questions are many. They do not have simple or easy answers. The very act of raising them,
however, is the critical first step to answering them.
The questions themselves point to the suspicions of
feminists about the connections between issues of
sexism and other injustices that permeate our culture. Like the intuitions that feminist clergy use as
signals to begin to explore events and situations more
deeply, these questions are only the beginning points
for long journeys of exploration and discovery in mission. Feminists know that the way we define the
questions will determine where we look for answers
and what assumptions underlie our sense of reality.
If we assume that our economic system is the only
viable system, we look for answers to poverty that
rely on the logic of that system. If we question the
system itself, new possibilities appear for resolving
the problems. If we believe that Christianity provides the only way to God's love and salvation, then
we are apt to define mission as bringing people to
Christianity. If we believe Christianity is one of several ways God has brought truth and love to our
world, then we look for ways to bond with others who
are on a common quest. Thus it is essential that we
hear our questions, for they will shape the ways we
formulate our mission.

Exposing idolatries

The mission of the church has been informed by the idolatries of our culture. While our country perhaps serves many false gods, two stand out as particularly urgent for the church's understanding of mission—equating the U.S. system of economics with Christianity, and our culture's consumer-oriented individualism. In the United States, the churches are bound up in a political and economic system that controls a massively unequal share of the world's power and resources. This system and its connections with multinational corporations is defended by our political and military system as the mainstay of freedom and Christian values. The quasi-capitalist economic system should be open to critique. It should not be an object of worship. Feminists who question this system know that economic power is not in the hands of the many but is held by a small elite. The fact of chronic unemployment and poverty in the richest nation in the world is often obscured by the myth of "equal opportunity," which blames the victim for her or his failure to "make it."[6] This system devalues the work of caring for children and domestic work. Feminists ask us to envision systems that place priority on taking care of our children by economically supporting that priority. Women have provided unpaid labor for childbearing and child care and have been used as surplus labor in the job market or as its lowest-paid members. Overall, women are still paid much less than men for comparable work. This is not an economic system that promotes the well-being and equality of women. It makes many women dependent upon men to support them, and it relegates many others to the margins of economic security.[7]

A second idolatry concerns the ways our culture reinforces a myth of individualism. Feminists have begun to uncover the biases that psychological theories and therapies bring to promote individualistic solutions to social problems, as well as the ways they perpetuate theories about the "feminine" and woman's nature that perpetuate an inferior status for women.

In the church, this emphasis on individualistic understanding of the self is embedded in definitions of sin. Sin is limited almost exclusively to personal behavior, rather than including corporate involvements in societal systems of injustice. The idea that the sins of the fathers really are visited upon the children is dismissed or used to perpetuate personal guilt, instead of revealing a condition of humanity that must be addressed. For instance, all whites in the United States inherit white privilege. That is a condition of reality to be challenged systemically. It cannot be eliminated just through personal repentance.

The church's counseling ministries have often perpetuated an individualistic, autonomous understanding of the individual's nature-in-community. The church has, sometimes unconsciously, sanctioned repressive family structures—for example, by assuming that the individual must be responsible for family disruption, rather than examining the family and even the culture itself for structural patterns of injustice. It has perpetuated a version of family life that encourages women's dependency and discourages men's role in sharing the maintenance functions and child-caring needs of family life. It can even lead to justifications for family violence. Clergywomen have found that it is not uncommon for clergy to assume that the basic solution to wife-beating is to counsel the woman to "work it out" and keep the family together. It is assumed that the nuclear family is God's intention for people, even when it is violent and repressive.

The white church will not be able to help change the social structure while it continues to participate in spiritualizing and individualizing the politics and power relations of people's lives, while it continues to have a disembodied spirituality that cannot face the real survival needs of people, and while it continues to project a ruling-class image of God as the white father in a hierarchical system. As long as these conditions prevail, success in the church will be equated with numbers and profit in a system where numbers, profits, and homogeneity are valued above the right to sustenance, justice, and mutual regard.

Clarifying commitments

The naming process is also important in clarifying commitments. Critical ethical and ideological conflicts often result, not from obvious conflict about general principles but in the specific naming of the content of those principles. Both antiabortion and pro-choice groups affirm the principle of the sacredness of human life. It is only in the naming process that one discovers *whose* life is sacred and *whose* issues are addressed. In feminist theory one cannot advocate justice without naming the issues in each context. To undertake this particularity of naming means that one's commitments have concrete expression and can be tested through concrete activity, thus providing information for reflection, critique, and accountability for one's activities. If we don't name the particular implications of our ethical and religious principles, we can escape responsibility for specific acts and we miss the opportunity to learn whether, in fact, what we profess makes any difference in what we do. The contexts in which we live out our commitments change and acquire new meanings and require new ways to be faithful.

Therefore, when feminists assert that Christian mission is carried out in acts of solidarity with the oppressed, they need to name not only what they understand the gospel message to be but also what it means for them in the context of their own church and culture. To take responsibility, as a witness in community, for naming signs of the new creation means taking the risk of making wrong choices—there is always the danger of equating new creation with one's own political establishment.[8] This is not just a danger for feminists, however. It is a danger for everyone. Feminists are deeply aware that they must live with ambiguity, be open to new insight, and refuse to claim ultimate authority even as they engage themselves with a whole heart in being witnesses.

To be a witness means to name and act upon one's political commitments. To give specific names to one's political and personal choices is to give concreteness to one's faith. To claim to love one's neighbor and to take no political action is to "spiritualize" one's witness, placing it outside effective concrete activity. In so doing, one closes off the possibility of deepening one's understanding of the meaning of love. To be a witness to God's promises means that by participating in liberating actions one can continue to reflect about the effects of actions. One thereby develops a basis for making wiser choices in a complex world. One learns what liberating activity is by participating in it.

For feminists, bearing witness through the power of liberating activity means at least to be treated as a subject, rather than an object, and to treat others that way; to struggle against any group or structure that denies people's own self-development and to widen and enhance people's opportunity to participate in shaping their own future; to understand that to witness is to be responsible and accountable to those most oppressed; and to affirm that everyone has the right to the essentials for survival. Bearing witness means, as Letty Russell says, to be on a long-term journey and lifetime struggle where there are no unambiguous answers, only clues to the promises of God. Witnessing always demands particularity—finding the right activity for the right context.[9]

This short introduction to the naming of questions, idolatries, and commitments from a feminist perspective only hints at the problems in defining the tasks of mission, but it indicates some of the concrete issues for mission and means, at least, working for fundamental change in the social, economic, and political system of the church and of the United States.

Service as empowerment

The commitment to fundamental change in the social and economic system in the United States means for feminists that to love God and neighbor one must give up power over people and help empower the victims of the culture and the system worldwide. In her book *The Socio-Theology of Letting Go*, Marie Augusta Neal says that the middle-class church in the United States needs to learn how to let go of its participation in an unequal share of the world's resources. It will have to examine its own life-style and structural involvements, she maintains, to help its members become conscious of their complicity in the system and learn how to relinquish unjust power and patterns of consumption.[10]

For feminists who agree with such critiques there are added complications. The language of servanthood in mission has often emphasized service as self-sacrifice. This is deeply problematic for women today. Sacrificial love language has often been used as an ideology to keep women subordinate to men. Feminists today are deeply suspicious of images of service and servanthood. Yet they are likely to agree with the critiques of Marie Augusta Neal and others about the privilege of white middle-class North American people and churches within the world context.

The women whose insights form the basis of this discussion are white and middle class. They are neither the poor nor the power elite. They are in the midst of what has been called a "dialogue of two positions."[11] They live in a sexist society and work with a church system that often denies their full humanity. At the same time, however, they live with the privileges that come from being part of a nation that maintains white privilege and class division. To be in solidarity, then, means to learn all they can about the connections between their own lives and the impact of their activities on others. Their "dialogue of two positions" must hold in tension their own marginalization and their participation in the domination of others.

For feminists the challenge is to address involvement in power over others and, at the same time, not be trapped into subservient roles. For instance, the idea of service has often been interpreted differently for men and for women. Men are given powerful roles—e.g., bishop—and called servants, while no servanthood role traditionally available to women carries any real power. By mystifying the concept of service, the church and society perpetuate self-denial in women, a self-denial that has already been fed by cultural denial of women's value and their creativity and needs. Women contend that the church hierarchy has traditionally used the concept of self-sacrificing love to keep women and other marginalized groups from challenging that hierarchy.

The history of domination of men over women has rendered women almost speechless in that they do not know how to talk about love, service, vulnerability, caring. Because of the dualistic nature of the language, women are caught within a language that construes self-assertion and self-negation as opposites. The inequality of power forces women, on the one hand, to fight for the validation of female experi-

ence but, on the other, not to reinforce dualisms of
care and conflict, of self-love and love of other, of the
feminine and the masculine.[12]

To broaden the understanding of mission, to drop
old baggage such as the expression "missionary en-
terprises," the clergywomen suggest certain words
and metaphors that have been empowering for them
in reflecting upon mission. One image from Ephe-
sians 2:11–22, that of God having broken down the
dividing wall of hostility in Jesus Christ, counters the
more sentimental image of "reconciling agents,"
which has been used as a reason to avoid conflict and
confrontation. To be in mission means we must break
down barriers before we reconcile. It suggests that
there are real dividing walls that must be confronted.
Struggle and conflict are involved when we engage
in a mission of justice. Another clergywoman talked
about using the image of the dog Toto in *The Wizard
of Oz.* As a woman in a church leadership position,
she compares her job to the work that Toto did in
pulling away the curtain, revealing the wizard as
human. The task is to help people realize that they
cannot leave their destiny up to the mighty gods—
false gods and fears—but must confront their illusions, expose the workings of the world, and not per-
sist in blaming the mysterious wizard for what
happens.

Others choose to reinterpret the language of service. Thus service, according to Ruether, needs to
be activity of reciprocity so that each person "actu-
alizes himself or herself by the same process
through which each also supports the dignity and
self-actualization of the other."[13] Therefore, to
serve is to work for a change in consciousness and
structures so that there are no servants, only sisters
and brothers. It demands a change in cultural sym-
bolism so that concepts of love are not sentimentalized. Service as empowerment means a change in
power relations. To live a life of service in this cul-

ture, women must demand equality in relationships and fight for economic and social changes so that some people do not have to be servants in order for others to prosper.

The language of service must also call people to own their power of personhood, their power of life itself, says Harrison.[14] The language of service must make clear that acts of service are acts of power that increase mutuality and one's ability to be in right relationship. Service does not imply pacifying others by acting for them but, rather, working with them to create shared power and shared resources so that all are empowered to shape their own destinies and all can be in mutual service.[15]

These women are also clear that they need to use what power they have. They are not to wait for a revolution, a majority decision, or church initiatives. They are always responsible for exercising the strength or talent or freedom they already have: to speak, to form organizations, to protest. They cannot remain passive because of what they do not have or because they fear to exercise power. They know that to participate in acts of solidarity does not guarantee success, but it does require that they start the movement toward liberation with whatever insight, act, or resistance they can bring.

This understanding of mission as a service of empowerment means that the task is not primarily to convert people to become members of the church. Rather, it is to engage in activity that shows people that God's gift of life is good. In Russell's words, it is to demonstrate that God offers "bread, not stones."[16] It means, she says, that the subject of our theology is liberating practice, not theology; the subject of the church's mission is empowering love, not the church.

In line with this understanding of service as empowerment, Harrison points out that the church is called to be involved where people have been disempowered, because, there,

what is authentic in the history of faith arises
only out of the crucible of human struggle. This
I take to be is the central, albeit controversial,
methodological claim of all emergent liberation
theologies. That the locus of divine revelation is
in the concrete struggles of groups and communities to lay hold of the gift of life and to
unloose what denies life has astonishing implications for ethics. It means, among other things,
that we must learn what we are to know of love
from immersion in the struggle for justice.[17]

Reconciliation—the promise of new order—only
comes when those who benefit from power over others give it up and when those who have been powerless are empowered.

To be in the empowering mission of the church
means to join in all struggles to overcome suffering,
to help people face the ways they are implicated in
their own oppression, and to work with them to resist
collaboration with that oppression. It means to call
for the just distribution of the world's good gifts so
that all can participate in mutual service, self-determination, and accountability to justice.

Mission in prophetic community:
Judgment and hope

Feminists believe that the church proclaims judgment and hope. The content of the judgment and
hope emerges as the combined voices of diverse peoples engage in acts of justice. Christians are part of
communities of struggle and hope that exist in the
midst of conflict and suffering. The Christian community is prophetic because its major task is to raise
consciousness about how we defile God's new creation, and it is a community of hope because it continues to move toward God's intentions. It names the
idolatries we serve and the sources of hope we have

for the future. The prophetic function begins within the community itself. It is the task of the community to formulate and reformulate itself as it engages in self-criticism. Because new voices need to be heard, because the social situation is in constant change, words and actions are provisional. The prophetic witness, according to Ruether, is first of all a self-critical voice.

> This means a constant struggle to clarify anew what established society always seeks to confuse. It means a constant effort to demystify the domestication of the messianic Kingdom which transforms prophecy into ideology and turns the revelatory instruments of judgment and hope into tools of self-sanctification and repression of criticism.[18]

Prophecy, because it contains judgment and hope, is pastoral care. Prophecy and pastoral care have often been seen as different functions in the church. Feminists contend, however, that each arises out of the other. In caring for one another, people cannot give up words of judgment. Deep caring for the other person involves honesty in areas of value differences and accountability to the other for one's actions. It means that in the midst of making judgments by engaging in action to oppose injustice, we cannot give up caring for the other person.

In this understanding of church, mission is shaped and reshaped as it seeks to address particular situations. It concerns the concrete, local struggles of persons to articulate the meaning of their lives and to be self-defining. It means joining others in the search for common goals. Our understanding of mission is in a constant state of reformation as we attempt to meet as equals in common commitment, nurturance, and celebration.

One of the major myths the church must work to overcome is that its mission, its commitments, and the private lives of its people can be separate issues. It is impossible for people to extend care to others and not get involved in politics, economics, and social conflict. It is false consciousness to claim this kind of separation. It leads to alienation and sentimentality.[19] The critical transformation of consciousness happens relationally. Thus, the church as a community needs to learn to question our world and to find ways to take action in the process of liberation. To do this the Christian community needs to counter many of the major assumptions of its life. It needs to be self-critical about its own class and racial contexts, and to look at its use of the earth's resources, as it joins in reconstructing the relationships between persons, groups, and the earth so that they are mutually supportive.[20]

This prophetic and hope-giving community needs to model new ways that people can support one another, ways that demonstrate not only how we might face pains and struggles in our community with love and compassion, but also how we might extend that care so that it is practiced in all spheres of society. The church has often been relegated to the private, family sphere. It needs to build advocacy for, and be a model of, ways to change the concerns of family life so that nurturance, child care, and maintenance functions are seen as public and political concerns. The church community must continue to struggle to be inclusive—not just by asking others into its life but by joining in acts of solidarity with others. Then an exchange of trust and mutuality might be possible based on common goals and interdependence, not on a desire for sameness or for lack of conflict.

As a start, the Christian community in the United States can exhibit care and justice in its own life, and it can articulate support of oppressed groups wherever they are found. The church learns to be faithful only by practicing faithfulness. There is no way to *prepare* to care or to join in solidarity other than through the process of caring and actions of solidarity. In Russell's examination of how people might learn to be partners—in her work in local congregations and seminary classes, and in her theological and biblical studies—she states that the most important thing she discovered was that people learn to be partners by *being* partners.[21] Hope is nurtured as it is practiced. The hope of the church in mission is reflected in its very style of being.

The prophetic and hope-giving communities need to have a plurality of structures to affirm what Russell calls the "riotous variety" of biblical images. These communities need to be pluralistic, to have the character of a movement, or journey, to find ways of interrelating that provide resources, power, and an ever-widening exposure to others, and to be flexible in structure so that specific structures are not identified with God's mandates.[22] In order to carry on the mission of solidarity with the oppressed, the church has clues, rather than a voice of authority, about what is needed. The church needs, therefore, freedom and courage to live with questions instead of expecting definitive answers. "In a changing world there are only changing answers."[23]

It is important to understand that the church as a prophetic and hope-giving community exists in a political, economic, and social system that needs radical reformation. Therefore, it will be on the border—a remnant community. It cannot expect to be of the majority until that majority has joined in the struggle for the empowerment of all. Aligning the church with the "least" continues to be an offense to the powerful. Even though the church is open to all, it cannot acquiesce to any form of injustice. Thus, the "rich young ruler" of Matthew 19 is invited on the journey, but he must make the choice of the path he follows.

As much as the church needs to repent and speak out against oppression and injustice, it also needs to embody concrete signs of hope. Clergywomen I spoke with especially emphasized that involvement in mission requires sustaining hope. Maintaining hope for participating in the creation of a new future is essential to sustaining mission over time. If people are to work to feed the hungry, provide release to captives, resist nuclear proliferation, fight injustice, and endure suffering, they must also remember the content of their hope, expect its incarnation, and experience moments, at least, of that hope in their time.

There are several ways women clergy sustain hope. It is important that people have a nurturing community that continues to tell the story of resurrection and the stories of the "saints" who have struggled to bring in new creation. For instance, stories of women have been a real source of hope for these women as they discover such friends as Anne Hutchinson, Judith in the Bible, Sojourner Truth, grandmothers. One woman said, "I could identify with them and so I know it's possible to make a difference because they did."[24] Another recounts the stories of the saints who "retain their courage, their humor, their sense of humanity, and their hope because it means we can too."[25] It is here, said one clergywoman, that the biblical stories can become stories about liberation, where "salvation history tells us that justice is a reality and love is possible and therefore it becomes known that the world is a place where substantial cultural, economic, and social change has to take place." People have actually undertaken this work before us and have shown us ingenuity, courage, and new life.

Second, they find possibilities for sustaining hope in the activity of common worship. Worship provides the weekly opportunity to voice the vision, to dream dreams, and to hold up our deepest values. It gathers the community together so that they can express truth in love to each other and find courage to face sin and evil. Worship is the time when the community shares hard issues. It is a time when people learn how to confront and to comfort. Hope is not built upon innocence, but upon the experience of facing pain and evil and learning how the community lives through crises with care and compassion.

The continual expanding of the boundaries of the community and of the life experiences of its members is a third way hope is sustained. If the hope these women cherish for new creation is to become a possibility, their visions must include the totality of God's world. Therefore, they believe it is important to develop and maintain local, national, and international connections in order to increase the depth of community, to share vital information about the world and each other, and to develop confidence gained from that sharing in making decisions about "mission" activities. They also prepare themselves through their activities for those moments when their particular gifts and resources might make a difference in creating a new world.

To sustain hope one needs to take seriously those parts of one's own culture that are signs of hope and use them. This means being cognizant of what resources are available and using them with as much power as possible. It means that, as women who share in the resources of the United States, we look for and expand upon the freedoms we do have, the information that is available, the access to resources that help mobilize people. For instance, one clergywoman came to realize how little she had exercised her ability to speak out about injustice just because she had become cynical about being heard. Then she went to South Africa and realized what it meant to have no voice at all. On returning to the United States, she vowed never again to underestimate the power she does have. Cynicism can become a form of apathy and denial of our own ability to act. As this woman said, "I was hiding behind my cynicism and not exer-

cising my hope." We need to strengthen those things
about our cultural heritage that we value. Hope is
sustained when we can affirm values out of our own
heritage.

A related way to sustain hope is what one clergywoman calls "adapting culture." To work in the
midst of the suffering of the world and the crises of
people's lives and sustain hope means "you are
counseling people how to adjust to that world. You
are adapting culture with them. You are creating
new vehicles for community life and are carving
out norms and values which actually enhance life."
The church structure needs to be creatively used to
strengthen links between oppressed peoples, provide access to resources, and be a place where people can practice different ways of being. The
church can provide alternatives to the "normal"
way to be. The church can begin changing gender
role work, ask people to do things they have never
done before, and help them learn new ways to be
in the world. It means developing a counter culture
that provides children and adults with new ways to
relate to each other. Thus, sustaining hope is never
an "abstract" disembodied task but involves using
all the resources of particular communities to carry
on concrete activities of hope. In sustaining hope it
is necessary to build church life and structures so
they become the sustainers of those who struggle
for life.

For these women, to sustain hope is to show how
the promised land is in our midst. One clergywoman
said, "We keep the ministry of Jesus alive by keeping
our covenants, re-creating community, and being
strengthened to do the work that re-creating calls
for, to sustain our devotion to God, to receive that
power, and to be as loving, as caring, as just, as merci-
ful and compassionate as we can be through all that."
As another clergywoman writes, it requires "practicing our hope":

In practicing our hope we trust that our vision of a New Heaven and New Earth will continue to nourish and motivate us. We trust our expressions of that hope will continue to move us closer to its realization. We trust that the energy of God's spirit will continue to surprise and sustain us. We trust that one day each of us, whatever our nation, class origin, race or gender, will participate as full persons in the kingdom promised each one whose *practiced hope endures to the end.*[26]

Unless hope is practiced, she continues, "one day we will find that we, too, have succumbed to the temptation to give up."[27]

Another clergywoman responded, "To engage in sustaining hope is not to engage in wishful thinking but to keep cores of people alive where people can covertly or overtly practice what self-determination means; to practice articulating priorities, to practice incarnating those responsibilities, and to inspire that hope for the future even if only a small core is alive to do it. Then human experience will not forget, and that possibility for life will not be erased from humanity."

Mission: Learning to act in solidarity

Learning to act in solidarity with people who are marginalized and oppressed is a difficult task, but it also gives these women energy to work constructively with crisis and suffering. For each clergywoman I spoke with, there are questions about particular actions and their meaning, but they affirm that acts of solidarity provide the source of much of their energy, hope, and motivation to fight conditions of oppression.

One of the major ways these women explore what it means to act in solidarity with others is by engaging in experiences that expand their consciousness, but which do not perpetuate patronizing and colonizing patterns as so many missionary endeavors of the church have done. They recognize that when "journeys collide," as has happened in certain situations, there are no easy answers to what solidarity with others means. They must make decisions about the use of limited resources, choose priorities, and make strategic decisions. Sometimes they find themselves in conflict with the very people they have chosen to stand with. Working through differences, misuse of power, and value conflicts is painful, but it is necessary if solidarity is to become more than a slogan.

To be in solidarity means for these women that they must learn again and again to have respect for persons with less access to resources or those who are oppressed by class, race, or sexual identity. They do not act initially to make friends or to be benevolent, but to treat others respectfully. Friendships between the oppressed and oppressors are a real and deeply important possibility, but friendship develops only out of mutual regard. It comes with the building of trust and long-term commitment.

In trying to expand both their own base and the community's base of experience, it is important to recognize that mutual sharing and concern must develop out of the ability for each person to recognize her or his own needs and to learn to care for others in ways that foster mutual liberation. One woman related her experience as chairperson of her conference social concerns committee. She discovered that people must first address the ways they actually connect to a social concern in their own lives—when discussing, for example, apartheid or homosexuality. They could then be more creative and energetic as a committee in addressing the public implications of these issues. If they first addressed their own feelings and experiences they could identify what actually informed their perceptions and analyses, and that increased their ability to explore ways of connecting life experiences. In this way, she learned that "the personal is political" also means "the political is personal." This approach to dealing with social justice issues suggests that we need to continue to explore real connections between what is often seen as an individual and personal issue and what seems to be an abstract issue of justice.

As whites, these women are conscious that their understanding of solidarity issues is based on their experience both of being among the exploiters in a world exploited by white Americans and of being women in a sexist culture. Their concerns about hope and solidarity come out of this double experience. They are concerned about white privilege and their own use of power over others. At the same time, they know that only in mutuality can life be fulfilled—not in their giving up the claims to the authority and responsibility for their own lives, but in learning to claim their own power as they work with others.

They have learned to listen to others' experiences, to search for connections and interrelationships, to be self-conscious of their own power and resources, and to use power to help others be empowered.

One woman talked about being in the mainstream "women's" culture and at the same time being a "token" clergywoman. "I work with those whose models of power I do not respect, and I work with those whose powerlessness calls me to be a good steward of power. . . . I work hard within structures, knowing that there are those who use me, trying to avoid being used where I don't want to be, but always seeking to make visible those who are invisible, raising issues where there has been a conspiracy of silence. I don't appreciate being called an Exceptional Woman in the midst of it. . . . I sort of feel like a wandering pilgrim down the road on this matter. I read all the signs around me, believing that there is the possibility of shared power, of solidarity. . . . It's still my best hope!"

Another important part of learning acts of solidarity is that these women ask themselves whom they choose to include as family and friends. In Matthew 12:48–50, Jesus asked, "Who is my mother? Who are my brothers?" Then he presented his disciples and said, in effect, "Look! Here are my mother and brothers! Whoever does what my Creator in heaven wants her or him to do is my brother, my sister, my mother." These women believe that, in saying this, Jesus was not denying the reality of his family of origin but instead was telling us that those whom we include as our mother, father, brother, and sister will deeply form our sense of what solidarity means. Those whom we choose to live with, those whose children we care for, those who form the intimate relations of our lives, will also form and inform our ways of being in solidarity. These people will form the network of personal care and accountability that becomes also the political connection we make with the wider world.

To be in solidarity means, therefore, finding ways to live "cross-culturally" so that our very being is involved in what happens to those who have less access to the resources of survival than we do. Many clergywomen have sought to do this in various ways. One woman is deliberate about her living situation, choosing to live in a part of town where she is confronted daily with the effects of a racist city. By doing so, she cannot forget racism; furthermore, she personally knows the conflicts, frustration, pain, energy, and courage demanded of ethnically diverse groups who live together. Another has deliberately chosen to work with women of color. She found that though white women talk about alliances, they have little experience of what that means. Her experience in this sphere has proven to be one of the greatest sources of energy in her own life.

"I would encourage women from one cultural perspective to form relationships with other women that are based on nonexploitative interchange over time; that these not be just projects that are done together, but that white women set their lives so that there is a way, over long periods of time, to engage in relationship. There are ways of giving and receiving and understanding what it means to be a woman in this world that can never be felt just by reading about it or hearing someone speak. Relationships of collegiality and friendship and shared struggle, where we have been able to carve out common priorities so that we can truly work together, have offered me some of the most profound relationships of my life and have garnered some of my deepest respect."

As with other aspects of their ministries, the ways women clergy sustain hope and act in solidarity depend upon the context of their community. If the community shares a sense of common vision and concern for justice and love, then the pastor's task is to sustain, prepare, and staff the mission efforts of the people. If the community has diverse concerns and goals, then the pastor will attempt to bring them into a sense of the common vision, or help those who share the vision of justice and love to sustain each other in a core group. If the community is powerful in the culture, then the mission task is to help expose the implications of power and call for responsibility-taking in their own lives. If the community is powerless, it means working to empower in ways that do not pacify or "do for." If the community is changing, it may mean assisting them to find a new vision that helps in change and readjustment and provides new vitality.

The concept of mission that these women share is directly related to their understanding of new creation and the issue of authority. New creation requires that all people should have the possibility to express their full humanity and participate in the gifts of life: sustenance, love, and community. The conditions for this new creation depend upon organizing intimate and political life so that justice and equality are available to all. The hope that sustains the community is the belief that all people can participate in fulfilling their own humanity if they have the opportunity to join in creating the new earth—in other words, if they can exercise their own authority.

The mission of the Christian church is, therefore, to work to create the conditions that will allow every person the chance to have the resources to meet material needs and the opportunity to participate in loving and being loved. To be able to live and to love requires justice and equality. The mission of the church is to participate in empowering the powerless. In participating in that struggle—in sustaining risk-taking, acts of courage, and visions—the people of faith also show forth in their life-styles the hopeful signs for a new humanity. The mission of the church is to be in solidarity with all oppressed persons and groups, not to convert them. Its task is to enhance the possibility of equality in the relationships it forms with others. It cannot determine other people's identities and meanings; it must affirm the belief that each group's experiences of meaning, if encountered with mutual respect and equality of power, are critical to the development of a new creation.

The church's task is to sustain the hope of new creation not by ignoring suffering and evil but by continuing both to work to create community and to act lovingly. The church must continue to search for ways to be in solidarity with all those who are victims and oppressed. Each community of Christians must name the principalities and powers of its historical time and place that suppress empowerment and justice. It carries out its prophetic function, not as the righteous community but as the caring community, as people who cannot remain silent in the face of suffering and injustice.

The content of mission is shaped through the daily struggles of people as they learn to survive and meet basic needs. The insight for mission strategy is dependent upon the "dialogue in the context." Said one clergywoman, "On one level, the issue of mission is very simple. It is proclaiming and acting out the good news of new creation. What is difficult is to examine the impact of what we're doing and what it means as we actually live it out. The dialogue in context is essential to understanding of the task."

"To act faithfully," said another clergywoman, "is to expect suffering, to learn patience, and to learn to be care-full in sustaining efforts over time. It means facing doubts about one's actions and being willing to change." The church community thus is not the new creation; rather, with its particular resources and visions, it participates in a common struggle with all who desire to create the new earth and new humanity.

Conclusion

Both the feminist theologians and the clergywomen state that the mission of the church is to participate in activity that empowers all who are poor, oppressed, or marginalized. This, they say, requires that we learn how to be in solidarity with people in ways that actually empower us all to become the makers of our own humanity and to create a common good. The feminists envisage the Christian concept of service not as servitude but as the process of empowerment in community. They inform us of the critical importance of "naming" in this process. By our language and the way we describe our realities and faith experiences, we have the power to obscure, distort, or clarify what is happening in our world. They emphasize that we need to be

involved in activities that nurture hope by embody-
ing qualities implied in the vision of new creation.

Feminist clergywomen stress the importance of
learning what solidarity means in the concrete life of
particular communities. They find insight into what
the mission of the church must be as they encounter
people struggling to survive and to meet basic needs.
They are dedicated to expressing professed values as
concrete activity. To advocate solidarity means for
them recognizing the power we already have and
then learning how to use it to empower. Furthermore, in their experience they find that solidarity
activity has to be embedded in nurturing and caring
relationships if that activity is to be sustained over
time.

Mission activity is always strategic, contextual, and
practical. It is practice that is constantly correlating
experience and values. The activity of mission
emerges out of the lives of particular people who
attempt truthfully to explain to those with whom
they act why they are involved, why they remain,
what it means to them, and what it costs.[28] It is something we do, not *for* others but *with* others, in the
mutual struggle for new life.

What Letty Russell says about learning how to be
partners, referred to earlier, applies also to learning
to be in solidarity. We will have to practice the art of
interdependence, of inclusion, of freedom. We cannot just declare ourselves committed to principles.
We will only learn what they mean as we practice
them in our daily lives. We must learn to practice the
ends we seek in the means we employ: first, because
means that are counter to the ends we seek form us
in their way of being, not in the ways we are trying
to learn to become; and second, because we do not
have to wait until some future time to participate in
the vision we hold. Through our acts of solidarity we
learn not only ways to empower each other but actual moments of empowerment, mutual love, all the

attributes of loving-kindness. When we achieve any-
thing at the cost of oppression and injustice, we hear
the Old Testament word of judgment:

> Woe to those who build a town with blood,
>   and found a city on iniquity!
> For the stone will cry out from the wall.
>   (Habakkuk 2:12, 11)

If we act for people but do not learn to be with them
in their dignity, pain, and beauty, we will discover
what Alice Walker, the poet and writer, tells us:

> (in answer to your silly question)
> people have eaten fried fish
> with the people
> sewn on sewing machines
> with the people
> assaulted school and church
> with the people
> fought feet to feet
> beside the people
> have given their lives
> to the people
> but they have forgotten to shout
> "i *adore* the people!"
>
> so the people's tribunal approaches.[29]

The mission of the Christian community is determined as its people experience solidarity—"being
with others"—in such ways that there is reciprocal
understanding of what liberating activity means.
Thus, mission is never totally defined by the Christian community but is informed and shaped in interaction with all who are engaged in liberating activity.

5

Vocation: Meaningful Work

The relation of work to Christian vocation is unclear
in both the biblical and the historical tradition. In the
Bible we encounter images of work as painful labor;
or as an expression of our talents; or as a task to feed
the poor, clothe the naked, comfort the afflicted, and
visit the prisoner; or as our special duty as slaves,
masters, women, men; or as justice-work. In the history of the churches, Christian vocation has sometimes meant a specific life-style (monasticism); sometimes it refers to the totality of every Christian's life,
and sometimes to the specific work of clergy. We are
the inheritors of a system that has traditionally honored the specialized vocation of the few, and at the
same time of a theology that implies that all Christians have a vocation. Within mainline Protestant-
ism, ordination has become the symbol of the unique
vocation of the chosen few. The Protestant emphasis
on the work ethic as a vocational issue, in its most
extreme forms, has been used to rationalize success
in the work world and to devalue those who do not
work.

Studs Terkel, who has recorded people's reactions
to their work lives, reports one person's reflection
upon her work: "I think most of us are looking for a
calling, not a job. Most of us, like the assembly line

worker, have jobs that are too small for our spirit. Jobs are not big enough for people."[1] This statement is especially poignant when we reflect upon Christianity's emphasis on vocation. Many jobs are "too small for our spirit." Many jobs are "not big enough for people." They do not enhance a sense of purpose or encourage particular talents. The division of work in our culture is unjust. Access to jobs is still conditioned by class, race, and gender. For many people, work has little connection to personal meaning except as a way of making money. Some work is terribly boring, hard, meaningless, and life-draining. Other work is creative, fun, and life-giving. Most work is done largely to ensure survival. The relationship that now exists between how much one gets paid, how significant the work is, and how meaningful it is to the individual seems irrational and most unfair. Some of the most important work that human beings do—caring for and nurturing children—is indirectly supported or not supported at all!

Christian understandings of work and its relation to call and vocation become especially significant for feminists. To understand the vocational concerns of feminists today, we need to see that there is a serious dual critique involved—the critique of the traditional roles for women within the church and the culture and, at the same time, a critique of the present roles of clergy and laity. In order to address vocational issues we need to first press further the implications of feminist understandings of the human person (or what the tradition has called "human nature")—especially the feminist understanding of the open-ended character of human freedom. Then we will look at the relationship of "call" to vocation and of vocation to work as it is presently structured. This leads to a discussion about ordination and how feminists who are clergy are struggling to redefine ministry.

Human "nature" and human becoming

Feminist critiques of the traditional and stereo-
typed views of the roles of women are well known.
Theories about human nature in general and female
nature in particular have shaped theologies of Christian vocation. Christian history has been dominated
by perspectives on female human nature that have
severely limited women's roles and their leadership
in the church. One of the most blatant examples is
the theory that woman's nature excludes her from
priestly functions. The theories about female nature
that have been used to justify such exclusion have
been determined more by historical and social
power arrangements than by any innate conditions
of biology, "scientific" theories about characteristics
of the feminine, or God-given commandments about
the proper relationships between men and women.

In our culture women's roles are largely determined by economic and social relationships. The por-
trayal of the sensitive and delicate Victorian lady
exists side by side with the reality of women who are
mill workers and farm laborers. Cultural and religious images of women have been used to justify
economic and political systems that are still being
used to exclude women from economic justice. Thus,
women continue to be paid less than men for their
work in the marketplace. Their domestic work and
child care have not been considered worthy of institutional and public support. As a result, women have
been dependent upon individual men or left to support themselves and their children.[2]

Feminists look critically at the history of women's
socialization to find causes for the place they have
been given in society. Women have begun to name
the economic and political realities that have created
the theories used to subjugate them. At the same
time, women are learning to value and respect those
parts of their experience that, though devalued by

the patriarchy, point the way to a new humanity. For instance, women are valuing the nurture skills they have learned. They refuse to limit these skills to personal life but bring them into the economic and political arenas. They know that they need to examine this human connection from their own perspective, to explore its complexities in light of its inherent value rather than out of an assumption that women need to be either less emotional or less objective. They are learning new ways to be both assertive and nurturing, rational and emotional.

Feminists critiquing traditional views of female nature also note that views of "nature" tend to be extremely *static.* Feminists state that this is contrary to their experience of the human condition. Experience and reflection upon history indicate that human nature is open-ended. As Letty Russell states, "We have to find our own provisional answers along the way as, through our decisions, we interact with our environment, and come to name ourselves and our world, taking responsibility for our lives. In this sense, human nature is an unfinished experiment."[3] Human activity transforms human nature. Therefore, one cannot appeal to any definition of human nature external to the process of developing human nature.

Furthermore, humans are formed within the matrix of relationships. One does not become "someone" outside the context of relationships. The quality of our interactions has the power to shape our humanity. It has the literal power of life and death. One knows that a newborn child depends on others for its survival. It cannot exist without others' care and nurture. The baby will die by itself. Human beings have the power to kill each other, as well as to care and love one another into life.[4] The question of who one becomes is always a question, therefore, of who one becomes *with others.*

Thus, one of the critical concerns is not to discover

what is human nature but to face the ethical question
of how people relate and what they choose to work
toward "becoming."

As feminists who believe that human nature is neither static nor biologically determined, these women
emphasize that people need opportunities to be self-
determining, they need access to the social and
political resources that can enhance that self-determination, and they need relationships of love and
mutuality to sustain possibilities for their own
becoming.

The possibilities of human nature will only be fully
known when all people can be creators in the process
of becoming. Until that time, the vision of what humanity might be is a partial vision because it lacks the
insight and contribution of whoever is excluded.

For these feminists a vision for a new humanity
that is glimpsed in the biblical tradition invites all
persons to participate, nurtures the quality of relationships, and sets forth the criteria of justice and
mutuality essential to the development of a new humanity. In this understanding of human nature, God
is seen as partner, as co-creator of the world and of
human meaning. As Letty Russell notes, "The relatedness of human persons is always situated in history,
and God's relatedness takes place in and through
history."[5] To be made in God's image means, therefore, that God's image is made manifest through our
participation in the project of creating a full humanity. In the process of being set free and setting free,
we practice God in our lives when we practice mutuality and support for our vision, creativity, and connectedness to each other.[6]

These reflections raise some serious and new concerns for feminists' perspectives on ministry. Several
intriguing feminist theories about socialization and
identity formation have become current—for instance, the psychological work of Nancy Chodorow
or the ethical theories of Carol Gilligan.[7] These theo-

rists argue that mother-dominated child rearing forms the identity of girls and boys differently because girls do not have to separate themselves from their primary care-giver in order to form their egos. Hence, such theorists argue, women always remain more attentive to the connections of relationships. Among other implications, this may mean that traditional ethical theories about autonomous persons and individual rights do not express women's ethical actions and perceptions adequately. Many feminists find these explanations of their experience and concerns to be powerful. Women do often find themselves emphasizing concrete nurturing activities and community-building, as do many of the women clergy I interviewed.

But there may also be serious traps here. It is often said that women clergy bring new gifts to the churches in precisely these areas. But that may box women into perpetuating traditional feminine roles. It may not represent liberation either for themselves or for other women. It may cut off possibilities of developing other styles and qualities. There are problems in our traditional socialization as women. While we affirm, for instance, our skills of mothering and nurture, we must also refuse to equate those skills with the female or continue the myth of male/female complementarity.

It is much more important to emphasize that these are the skills and qualities of marginalized persons, who must be more alert to the subtle signals of body language and emotional well-being than those who are in power. As Carter Heyward put it in reflecting about her journey toward ordination:

> Our transforming power is not inherent in our gender, for we are simply human, like our brothers. Our power lies in our having been born, nurtured, and acculturated into a corporate symbol: a symbol not necessarily of "femininity,"

but rather a symbol of *difference.* Together, we
offer a difference to the church, a difference that
includes the corporate experience of exclusion,
and the particular experiences of being daugh-
ter, wife, mother, lover, and the various other
roles we have played.[8]

Other women emphasize wholeness, or liberation, or
process. But the point is similar. Even as we embrace
who we have been, as devalued and marginalized
women in a sexist society, we must be wary of em-
bracing previous sexism as it was. We need to understand ourselves also as women who are creating ourselves, making decisions about who we are becoming
and will become. Our female activity transforms female nature as surely as any human activity transforms human nature. We are on journeys that are not
yet finished, and that are full of new possibilities from
which we learn as we go.

Therefore, feminists challenge any concepts of vocation that use past socialization or gender as major
criteria for determining woman's place, function, or
"natural" attributes. It is within this open-ended understanding of what we are becoming that these
feminists address the concepts of call and vocation.

The universality of call
and the particularity of vocation

One of the most basic issues in understanding ministry has been the relationship between the common
ministry of all Christians and what has been called
the "specialized call" to ordination or "set apart"
ministry. In order to gain some clarity about vocation, I will separate the issue of call from vocation
and then relate both to ministry.

The clergywomen acknowledge that they had a
strong sense of call. They did not find, however, that
their sense of call was to a particular job; it was, as one

said, "becoming who you were meant to be." What people are called to, then, is not a specific job but a willingness to move ahead through their life with the sense that it has meaning and purpose. They are called not only *out of* who they are, but *to* who they are becoming. Some women talked about the spiritual dimension of this experience of call as being akin to an energy source that moves them forward. One recounted her experience when she resisted this sense of call: "I can't stand what happens to me when I don't move ahead. I have a sense of what I have to do and feel it as an urge. When I've resisted it, I become physically ill. However, to talk about this experience is always to risk being seen as arrogant or weird, instead of integrated and connected. Because status and power are attached to particular jobs, it is difficult to express one's deepest feelings without those experiences being seen as 'special' calls."

The women recognize how difficult it is to talk about a sense of call because it is used, said one, "as a double-edged sword" within church structures. There, call is often understood as a special and unique sign from God that comes to the chosen few, illustrated by the question, "Are you really called by God?" rather than anyone's deep, spiritual sense of response to life that is profound but available to all. As these women understand call, all people are called to fulfill their humanity.

The "call" for Christians means to become part of the people who find Jesus and the Gospel stories to be compelling for their sense of life's deepest meaning. As one said, "So far as we are walking in the steps of that calling, that is Christian calling." Not only are we responding to a sense of being called, we are accepting responsibility for our life. Call, another explained, is both a response to and a "responsibility for one's own creativity and life's meaning." To live as a called person is to be responsible for the integrity of one's life, to struggle against whatever forces deny the fullness of being. Said one, "My sense of call wouldn't change if I weren't a clergyperson. Being a clergyperson doesn't make me different from anyone else who responded to the call, just one who has a different work."

For these Christian feminists, the call is to a way of life and to the commitment to a vision. The call is to all Christians equally. All Christians are called to express their faith experience and to use their gifts in proclaiming the good news of that faith. To be called by God means "to express, embody, share, celebrate the gift of life, and to pass it on."[9] The call is to the whole Christian community. The issue for Christians is the *integrity* of the response, not the uniqueness of the call.

The ability to relate the call to specific vocations involves a more complicated process. Whereas no one can be denied her or his sense of call, vocational identity is developed through a process of discernment and expressed within the opportunities and limitations of particular contexts. One's vocational identity is shaped within the matrix of specific talents, the historical context, and the demands and needs of particular places; it depends on the physical and spiritual resources that are available. One's vocational identity can change over time. It is conditioned by a complex interaction of accidents of birth, historical events, and relationships, as well as one's own sense of creativity and needs.

Vocational expression is linked to community support. In order to get clarity about one's own gifts and talents, one needs the insight, feedback, and nurturance of others. It means, as one clergywoman said, "a willingness of people to share perceptions with each other. In order for someone to get vocational clarity, others need to recognize that person's talents, testify to those gifts, and support and nurture them."

The expression of one's gifts is always related to

one's relation-in-community. Christian communities are called to support, confront, critique, and affirm the expression of gifts, and it is the community context that makes the individual expression meaningful. Because people are rooted in relationships to others, the expression of each person's creativity is bound up in those relationships. *People are not self-made.* As in the Christian analogy of the body of Christ, no particular part can function on its own. Likewise, any damage to a part affects the healthy functioning of the whole. However, the image of the body of Christ also cannot be static. Sometimes it has been used to limit the possibility for people to have changing roles in community. Whereas the imagery implies that we are preordained to be a particular part, as in "once a toe, always a toe," in reality we are creating the body as we go. The body-of-Christ imagery must include the possibility of a new creation emerging.

The Christian community has several responsibilities in the vocation-defining process. First, as one clergywoman said, "It must guard against creating a hierarchy of values where some gifts are worth more than others." Second, the community has the responsibility to nurture the fragile development of self-identity, to affirm differences, and to form the connecting links that show how different talents actually increase the value of the whole. Finally, the community must analyze the social and economic realities by paying attention to both the survival needs of its members and the possibilities for the best use of each one's talents.

Vocational identity is related to place, time, and needs.

One clergywoman stated, "I'm not one who believes in career—I believe in vocation; therefore, I cannot predict where you are going to find me or us a few years from now. We need to be open to vocational reshaping. I'm very much against the concept of people just heading for a particular form of ministry such as the pastorate or a hospital chaplaincy. I feel that people should be flexible as to where they can be."

Said another woman, "I don't equate vocation with my job as a clergyperson. Sometimes when I was working outside the church and doing volunteer work in the church, I felt I did more ministry than I do in many parts of my job as clergy. Sometimes I feel as clergy that a lot of work that I do is not relevant to my particular sense of vocation or its impact, even though the job is good work and needs to be done."

These women pastors are conscious also that in any community the limitations of people's resources and the imperatives of their needs shape the realities of vocational choice.

"Sometimes it seems that pastors tend to blame individuals for their choices, without looking at the contexts and the issues of power. While it is very important to affirm the possibility of choice and change, it is destructive to set up criteria for what is valued, if people are denied access to resources or must meet other responsibilities."

Yet the community also has some responsibility to indicate how talents should be used. As one woman said, "Sometimes, in spite of its many dangers, I want the church to say, 'We bless these vocations; we don't bless those,' to make judgments about the ways people spend their lives." These women recognize that with judgment also comes the responsibility to point to alternatives and help create new options for work. They recognize that what actually results from the vocational choices we make is never totally within a particular person's or group's control. We are also informed by where we find ourselves.

"I was shaped by the fact that I was the only woman among the clergy in my conference and had to pave the way. That has defined what I am a lot and it will continue to affect my ministry more than I want it to many times. . . . I would like to have more control over what issues I deal with but have to deal with the fact of being a *woman* in ministry."

Finally, in discussing issues of vocation, these women were all conscious that their own life choices depended also upon their color, their access to education, their nationality, and the supportive relationships in their own lives. Therefore, they recognize that even to suppose that vocation is linked to choice and nurture of talent is an assumption that comes from a privileged position in a world where vocational choices are often subsumed in issues of survival.

Thus, for these women, vocation is not settled when one chooses to seek ordination. Vocation remains an open question about the shape of one's life and the integrity of one's response to God and others—not because one is neurotic or has unresolved issues but because vocational direction has to be periodically reexamined. For many of these women the deepening sense of clarity raises, in a sense, new ambiguities and conflicts. The misunderstandings and conflicts that exist around certain work do not go away just because an individual finds vocational clarity. The social base of work remains, and basic contradictions may become more visible as women become clearer about their vocational direction.

I did talk with these women about the particular journeys by which they came to ordination and the parish. As with any group of clergywomen, their paths were varied.[10] Some were clear that their vocational talents led to work in local churches. Some were on a broad religious search that led them to seminary and gradually to ordination. But while these pathways may be interesting to explore, they were not the major concern of these women as we talked about vocation.

Rather, they were far more concerned with issues about how they came to identify and value themselves and their gifts, and to realize that these gifts were useful and needed. Often they felt that, as women, they had received little feedback about their skills and gifts. The sexist society and church under-values and trivializes women's gifts and contribu-tions, or values them only as they relate to the pri-vate sphere.

Furthermore, the realization of these women that they had valuable gifts was not an isolated event. Through their own experience of choosing a vocation that is not a usual one for women, they began to recognize that *everybody* has gifts that are needed and that need expression. The self-realization of vo-cation for these women was integrally connected to a realization about community and about the injus-tice of undervaluing and negating the gifts of all be-lievers. Their greatest concern, therefore, was not in the items many sociologists or other observers of clergywomen seem to find important. It was the strong theological affirmation that all people, no mat-ter how marginalized or negated, have valuable con-tributions to make and creativity to offer. It is crucial to these women's experiences and understandings of vocation that we must struggle to honor the gifts of all, to enable all people to express these gifts, and to change the conditions that trivialize them.

Ordination

It is with these understandings of call and vocation that feminists examine the role that ordination has played in the life of the church. As Ruether explains:

> When Constantine made the Christian Church the official religion of the empire, the Christian ministry [ministry = clergy] was established as a social caste and received the privilege tradi-tionally reserved for the pagan priesthood of the official cultus.[11]

The functioning of clergy as a caste system, according to Ruether, has continued through the Reformation to the present time in spite of attempts to develop a theology of the "priesthood of all believers." This caste system has been maintained by a sexist and patriarchal hierarchy—which, despite revolts against the church hierarchies, continues to be modeled after the ruling classes of their society.[12]

In the United States the mainline Protestant church has often identified with the major structures of the society. Nevertheless, the clergy often feel cut off from viable public roles in society. They are generalist professionals in a highly specialized professional class. They deal largely with women and children. They are often overworked and dependent upon the laity in churches for their income. Yet from the lay perspective, the clergy are still part of a system that perpetuates hierarchy and "sets apart" the ordained to perform the holy sacraments and to "represent" the church.

For feminists this hierarchical, set-apart clerical pattern is dysfunctional for the white Christian community. In spite of church theories about servant leadership and the enhancement of the role of the laity, feminists find that many churches continue to perpetuate a caste system. Laity often see the clergy as the real ministers, and many clergy and laity equate call and Christian vocation with ordination.

Therefore, Russell declares, for those who choose to work within the ordination system, the task is to "subvert the clergy line." While many of the functions and tasks of ministry are critical in our time, no particular group should have "special" privileges to perform any function. She claims that the goal of clergy should be to "go out of business" by empowering the total community to carry out the ministry. Clergy should not assume that any function is automatically theirs. Rather, in working to enhance the gifts of all, they may find that other people become preachers, that sacraments might best be carried out communally, and that theologians might work best from within local communities, rather than in separate institutions.[13]

Clergywomen feel a deep sense of call and find vocational satisfaction, energy, and excitement in the role of local church pastor. Yet ordination brings contradictions. They see it as a functional issue. Though their talents are used in this role, they do not see ordination as necessarily a "for life" decision. As one woman explained, "To leave the parish ministry as a pastor is not to leave the ministry. The only way one does that is to leave the Christian community." The women's sense of vocation is not tied to being ordained. They consider it much more healthful and creative if people are able to be flexible in their job decisions. At some points it might be better to change jobs. In the context of the community, one needs to assess particular work regularly and not hold that "what I do today is what I should do tomorrow."

They recognize that, in fact, ordination does influence the way they are perceived, especially the way people give them access to their lives and to their greatest fears, pains, and suffering. They do not dismiss these gifts of openness. For them, the issue is not to deny the value of such relationships or the power they have, but to extend the possibility that other people of the community can also be seen as trustworthy and as having resources and strength for each other in times of crisis. In that sense, the clergyperson is no more a "representative" than anyone else who identifies with the community. The issue, as one put it, is how "we *all* model with and for each other the meaning of our lives."

Nevertheless, the institutional and cultural baggage attached to the role of clergy means that there are contradictions in the theory and the practice. Says one, "What I do or say carries more weight now that I'm ordained. It means that my statements are supposed to have more integrity and authority than those of the average layperson." They are not naive about the power of the role, and they recognize that while they strive to change it, they also need to recognize the anomalies of the present situation. Some of the women pastors have to be careful about where and with whom they seek counsel and support for the intimate issues in their lives. They are sometimes perceived as "other" because their role is experienced by people in their congregation in ways that do not dissolve just because the pastor declares all are sisters and brothers together. They must deal with the present realities while engaging to change the perceptions that clergy partake of the holy in ways other people do not. They work toward a time when all in the church honor their own sacredness and that of others.

This understanding of ministry means that for these women pastors, at present, the work of the clergy is to empower the ministry of the whole. Several women recounted their anger at predecessors in their churches who had pacified and disempowered the laity.

Said one, "The former clergy made all the decisions for this church and the part of people which wants other people to make their decisions for them was reinforced. I have a sense that they have been ripped off in the past by clergy, put down, not validated, not confirmed. I cannot describe the rage I felt when I came here at some of the work of my predecessors."

In church situations where the laity have been disempowered by either the society or the clergy, the major function of these women clergy has been to work for common empowerment and to refuse to be the ministry for people. Several said, "I stress in my work that I could not be the church, that all of us would have to struggle with the issues." Said one clergywoman, "I refuse to make decisions for them. I will lead but will not determine the direction by myself. It works; it's slow; they've had twenty years of disempowerment. First they thought it was my inexperience that kept me from making their decisions; now they actually name it as empowering them."

Said another woman, "I like being part of the community and am willing to take responsibility for my work when my role is clearly there. But the local church is their church. It shouldn't be a crisis to change clergy and it doesn't have to be if they are doing the work themselves. It does make the work of clergy more complicated."

This understanding of their work as empowerment is also reflected in the women's comments about their function in the counseling role. They said, "The issue is to help people make their own decisions; to be able to hang in with people in times of crisis and not succumb to making decisions for them." One woman said, "When I counsel, I always pay attention to the power issues involved. It is important to know what social, economic, and political power a person has in order to understand an essential part of the counseling issue." Clergy are too likely to become decision makers for others when they do not recognize the power that others invest in them in the counseling situations.

In churches where the laity do have economical, political, and social power, the clergy's job is to find ways to bring laypeople together to share their knowledge and acknowledge their responsibilities. The task is to help them understand that religion does not only relate to their "personal" lives but that it also helps them see the connections between what they do and what happens in the world.

A second function of the clergy that is consistent with the issue of empowerment is to develop collegial and teamwork situations. It is important to the clergywomen to share leadership roles and develop team working relationships in order to practice their understanding of the ministry. Because these women find the basic institutional structure unhelpful in promoting team ministry or collegiality, they have "improvised" in different ways. In one setting, all the clergy staff work part-time in the church and part-time elsewhere. This arrangement both creates a working team and brings in the finances to make it possible. Others have spent much time in developing lay leadership so that they have "working teams" for specific functions. One woman who worked in an interracial situation strove to make sure that she had a multicultural pastoral team. She recruited ethnic minority seminarians and, as far as possible, provided them opportunities to work as co-pastors. Others deliberately seek women's groups both in and outside the church where they can share their sense of commitments and struggles so that they do not become "loners" or "one-woman operations." The women also discussed the important distinctions between working one's way out of the job of being "the ministry" for the church and, on the other hand, the possible misuse of that goal as an excuse for not doing one's work.

Therefore the challenge for these women is to work toward the time when the understanding of ministry includes the expectation that every Christian will come to vocational clarity. There are many small but concrete and important changes that could be made in order to make the "priesthood of all believers" a reality in the lives of people. For instance, presently ordination is a highly symbolic, public affirmation of the vocation of the clergy. These celebrative occasions, however, also implicitly mark the ordained person off from other Christians. It is important to develop rituals for the "ordination" of every Christian. The community can then be responsible for affirming and holding them accountable to their vocation. The local parish can encourage people to share their vocation-work-job concerns and issues in the church. We can inquire about jobs and how work relates to their faith and their understandings of vocation instead of passing over these things in silence. Meanwhile, we need to find ways to be able to speak to present realities of people's lives in such ways that we do not perpetuate cynicism or loss of self-worth and dignity; that we do not spiritualize away the real conditions of work or demean or victimize those who work to survive. We must increase the real possibilities for all to have creative and meaningful work to do.

Ministry

Ministry does not refer to the work of clergy but to the activity of all Christians as they live out their sense of vocation. Ministry is what enables people to live their commitments and express their understanding of the source of their identity and meaning. As one clergywoman said, the ministry involves the struggle "to search for a common good, where people understand what it is to be moral, to be committed, to be faithful, to give thanks and glory for the sources of their lives and energy, to struggle against and to transcend pettiness, jealousy, and the narcissism of their lives."

Over time, certain functions in sustaining community have taken on great significance in the Christian tradition: forms of worship life, sacraments and rituals, education and nurturance functions, common mission activities. In this process the work of ministry has often become associated with the role of the clergy. Women pastors reject this understanding of their work. Depending upon their specific context, they have different emphases in their particular functions, but all are clear that they are not the ministry. The ministry belongs to the people of the community.

The development of a common faith includes the right and the responsibility of all members to reflect upon their experience of the faith and to be open to each other's faith expressions. "To share one's own faith experience with others is *the religious function,*" said one clergywoman. For Christians this means to develop an identity as the people of God as they explore their faith tradition, the Bible, the stories of saints, and their own revelations. They see in their own activity part of God's incarnation—God's body in this world.

The ministry of the community is experimental and experiential. It hopes to encourage people, said one, by being a place "to experiment with new behaviors, a place where you can learn what you might be if you were a little different and what you might do differently in work, family, and so on." It is the attempt, said another, to "share concerns and issues with people who make available the time to listen to those who hurt, . . . make space on their calendars for particular activities, . . . make space in their spirits for particular concerns."[14] The ministry of the church is to develop both collective activity and support for risk-taking wherever people try to incarnate God's mercy and justice. Thus, it needs to be experimental.

In sharing faith experiences, the ministry of the church takes on its experiential character. In the gathering of the collective talents, care, and wisdom, the experiential nature and the creative bonding of the people of God becomes possible. One woman reports:

> Not only do we recognize that, however important the specific work of isolated individuals, most of us can work effectively over a long pe-

riod only when that work is undertaken with the
support and shared effect of others having similar concerns. The longer I remain in this parish,
the less I am preoccupied with "mobilizing" others and the more I am committed to participating in a common struggle rooted in an identifia-
ble community of people.[15]

Each community has to determine its own particular function in its culture. It cannot rely on any one
description of what Christian ministry should be. In
one place the community may be called to resist
oppression; in another it may be called to relinquish
some of its wealth; in another to comfort. Within any
Christian community, because all gifts are needed
and depend upon mutual functioning, there should
be no hierarchy of functions or gifts.

The image of service is still a powerful symbol for
feminists, as we have seen in the previous chapter.
Yet the concept of a ministry of service continues to
be used to disempower laity, especially women, and
to mystify clergy use of power by calling it servant
leadership. In order to change the concept of ministry being associated with clergy, we recall Letty Russell's suggestion that all who are in ministry should
take on the role and language of partnership.[16]

Accordingly, for these women, God empowers, not
like a "big leader," not as the one who calls particular
people to "holy" orders, but as one who serves to
empower the broken.[17] Jesus warns that religious
leaders tend to become hypocrites, to want to have
places of honor at the feasts, to be greeted respectfully and addressed with a title ["pastor" would be a
modern example] (Matt. 23). The *ministry* is
the activity of the community of faith. It is not the
work of "representative" individuals. One can have
a clear sense of personal call and vocational identity,
but one participates in the common ministry of the
community.

These understandings of work and vocation recognize the unique gifts of individuals and the common tasks of the whole community. They assert that people want significant work, work large enough for their spirits. The vision for the Christian community is that it will become a place where all will find the encouragement and empowerment needed to express their gifts in the common ministries of love and justice.

6

Feminist Ministry: Vision of Friendship and Solidarity

The Christian feminists whose voices I have tried to hear and interpret in this book have lived with the pain of what Christian theologies and Christian history have done to women: namely, denied women's experiences of the sacred and crippled their well-being. Yet these clergywomen have also found enough life, vision, and sustenance to resist patriarchal and sexist forms of Christianity and to refuse to let them be authoritative for their lives. Instead, these women are finding empowerment by claiming their own authority to image and create new ways of being part of Christian communities that honor women's experience and that care passionately for women's well-being. In their experiences of salvation and in their activity in mission, they are attempting to sustain a sense of vocation that recognizes that creativity and passion as they work within and outside churches.

Two images of ministry are emerging: friendship[1] and solidarity. They do not attend to all dimensions of ministry, but they do help us break out of some destructive patterns and give us clues for incorporating the insight that the personal is political and the political is personal. They connect us to parts of our tradition and help us image a new future. "This notion of the ministry of friends returns to mind and

heart again and again," reports one clergywoman.
Said another:

"As we talk about the need for team ministry, I
have come to appreciate all the more my circle of
friends. They are the ones with whom I meet to reflect spiritually and theologically. They each bring
out a better me, and I believe I do the same for
them. We've cried together, laughed together, engaged in outrageous hysteria, confided in each
other, and stimulated each other's thinking and
creativity. We are friends with God in these encounters. Friendship demands honesty within one-
self and between each other. It demands risking
from me in totally new ways. Within the congregation I am learning to be friends with people. I know
that my well-guarded tendency is to say, "You fool,
you'll just get burned." But vulnerability is part of
friendship. What I do know is that nothing is to be
gained in the old model of power. Without friendship ultimately we have nothing, we gain nothing,
we lose everything. So I'm concentrating on what it
means to be friends—to cross clergy-lay boundaries,
to be friends with those who are different, and, as a
friend to God, to be counted as trustworthy, honest,
and accountable."

As we explore ways to understand our relationships to others and to God, friendship suggests both
the emotional intimacy we need and the mutuality,
nurture, trust, and accountability that we value. The
most powerful and best friendships we have give us
insight into love that implies reciprocity and an authority of selfhood that neither demands the other's
acquiescence nor makes the self subservient. It does
not deny uniqueness, nor does it require hierarchy in
order to be functional. Friendships are not limited by
kinship or culture. In friendship we find comfort and
sustenance in times of pain and sorrow. Friends give
us courage in times of risk-taking and danger.
Friends are people with whom we eat, laugh, and

play just for the great joy we share in each other's presence.

The friendship of Ruth and Naomi recounts the power of such feelings to inform and shape lives. The development of Jesus' relationship with his disciples came to the point where he told them that they were not to be servants, but friends. As his friends they shared in his knowledge of God, and as his friends he expected them to do even greater things than he had done. The power of the love of friends can even lead us to risk our lives.

The vision of church as a community of friends provides us with lived experiences that suggest ways to restructure church life.

Friendship suggests interdependence, mutual care, and genuine regard for the other's gifts. Friendship retains the affection-generating feelings that are so often mystified in descriptions of "agape" love that somehow suggest we transcend personal feelings. It also counters some of the parent-child concepts of love that keep us immature in the faith community.

For friendship to grow we need to become trustworthy and steadfast, people who can be counted upon in good and bad times. At the same time, friends can let each other see their vulnerabilities and weaknesses and can be challenged to change and can be forgiven.

As friends in community we take on responsibilities and accountability, but our roles can shift as our gifts emerge and as our common needs are defined.

As we seek to deepen friendship we find our very beings rooted in deep emotions of care. To be friends with each other, and to experience the friendship of God, roots community in the intertwining of body, soul and spirit.

Solidarity with all who are oppressed, poor, or silenced requires that we structure our social and political commitments to expand our visions and counter our parochialisms. Solidarity calls us to ac-

count for our use of power. According to Jon Sobrino
and Juan Hernandez Pico,

> Solidarity is another name
> for the kind of love
> that moves feet, hands, hearts,
> material goods, assistance, and sacrifice
> toward the pain, danger, misfortune, disaster,
> repression,
> or death
> of other people
> or a whole people.
> The aim is to share with them
> and help them rise up, become free,
> claim justice, rebuild.[2]

Solidarity requires consciously motivated activity
to change relationships of inequality and injustice. It
seeks economic and political empowerment to transform systems of oppression. Solidarity asks us to
honor the dignity of all persons and to resist any who
exert power over others. Solidarity grows out of our
sense of outrage at inflicted pain and unequal distribution of basic survival needs. To be in solidarity
with others does not require that they become like
us, but that together we give voice to all who have
been silenced, so that our experiences of mutuality
can be expanded and justice can truly exist. Desire to
be in solidarity moves us to assess any institutional
form that systematically represses or excludes particular groups of people. It leads us into concrete action
because it requires placing ourselves with those most
marginalized. It is a life-style that moves us toward
the victimized and challenges individualistic concepts of salvation. It calls forth the freedom we have
to resist and change injustice. Solidarity allows no
separation of the spiritual and the political.

As we seek to develop forms of ministry consistent
with feminist visions, the image of friendship and
solidarity can provide us with insight into ministry.
Friendship can give us the deep emotional bonding

that helps us endure, gives us joy, and strengthens our building of a relational life. Solidarity channels our activity of concern into structures of accountability to and empowerment of all who are oppressed.

We are only beginning to appreciate the depth and breadth of the transformations occurring as women begin responding in new ways to their experiences of the holy in our midst. Some of these elements have been raised here. However, they are suggestive and need the confirming practice, discernment, and reformulation of many women. They call us into new explorations of the struggles and possibilities that feminist visions of friendship and solidarity suggest.

In joining with women of faith and courage, our hope is to become Christian communities that will be signs that all can nourish and feed each other: *communion;* that all have a necessary and unique word to give: *proclamation;* that all have a vocation to fulfill: *empowerment.* As we work for communities of friendship and solidarity we embody the hope that we can dare to care passionately for each other, be vulnerable, and forgive each other. We live out, in different contexts and in fragments of time, expressions of the vision of relationships of loving mutuality and justice.

Notes

Chapter 1: Why Feminist Ministry?

1. Beverly Wildung Harrison, *Making the Connections: Essays in Feminist Social Ethics,* ed. by Carol S. Robb (Boston: Beacon Press, 1985), pp. 233–234.

2. H. Richard Niebuhr, *The Purpose of the Church and Its Ministry* (New York: Harper & Brothers, 1956). He claimed that the new metaphor for ordained ministry would be "pastoral director." Whether or not this title is descriptively accurate, it seems to have caught almost no clergy fancy. It pointed to the work that most clergy find less than motivating and often oppressive—administration and management. See the results of a study reported in Gerald J. Jud, Edgar W. Mills, Jr., and Genevieve W. Burch, *Ex-Pastors: Why Men Leave the Parish Ministry* (Philadelphia: Pilgrim Press, 1970), p. 41.

3. Donald P. Smith, *Clergy in the Cross Fire: Coping with Role Conflicts in the Ministry* (Philadelphia: Westminster Press, 1973); Jeffrey K. Hadden, *The Gathering Storm in the Churches* (Garden City, N.Y.: Doubleday & Co., 1969), p. 212.

4. The following are examples of this emphasis on the arts and skills of professionals: David S. Schuller, Merton P. Strommen, and Milo L. Brekke, eds., *Ministry in America* (San Francisco: Harper & Row, 1980); Samuel W. Blizzard, "The Minister's Dilemma," *The Christian Century* (April 25, 1956), pp. 508–510; James Glasse, *Profession: Minister* (Nashville: Abingdon Press, 1968); Robert G.

Kemper, *The New Shape of the Ministry: Taking Accountability Seriously* (Nashville: Abingdon Press, 1979).

5. Henri Nouwen, *The Wounded Healer* (Garden City,
N.Y.: Doubleday & Co., 1972). Two other books that give
insight into this concern are Daniel Day Williams, *The
Minister and the Care of Souls* (New York: Harper &
Brothers, 1961), and Henri Nouwen, *Creative Ministry*
(Garden City, N.Y.: Doubleday & Co., 1971).

6. Urban Tigner Holmes, *The Future Shape of Ministry:
A Theological Projection* (New York: Seabury Press, 1971).

7. Colin W. Williams, *Where in the World: Changing
Forms of the Church's Witness* (New York: National Council of Churches, 1963), and George W. Webber, *The Congregation in Mission* (New York: Abingdon Press, 1964),
are early examples of this approach to ministry. More recent writings include work by liberation theologians
around the world.

Chapter 2: By What Authority?

1. Elsie Gibson, *When the Minister Is a Woman* (New
York: Holt, Rinehart, & Winston, 1970), p. 152.

2. Sheila D. Collins, *A Different Heaven and Earth* (Val-
ley Forge, Pa.: Judson Press, 1974), pp. 31–45. See also
Frantz Fanon, *The Wretched of the Earth*, tr. by Con-
stance Farrington (New York: Grove Press, 1965). Fanon's
book develops the theory about why people in subordinate relationships find it difficult to validate their experiences and how they learn to live in two worlds of "reality."

3. Rosemary Radford Ruether, *Sexism and God-Talk:
Toward a Feminist Theology* (Boston: Beacon Press, 1983),
pp. 18–19.

4. Ibid., pp. 12–13.

5. Beverly Wildung Harrison, *Making the Connections*
(see ch. 1, note 1), p. 13.

6. Ibid., p. 13.

7. Ibid., p. 16.

8. Adrienne Rich, *On Lies, Secrets and Silence: Selected
Prose* (New York: W. W. Norton & Co., 1979), p. 193.

9. Letty M. Russell, *Growth in Partnership*
(Philadelphia: Westminster Press, 1981), p. 73.

10. Rosemary Radford Ruether, "Basic Communities:

Renewal at the Roots," *Christianity and Crisis* 41 (Sept. 21, 1981), pp. 235–236.

11. Harrison, *Making the Connections,* p. 262.

12. Russell, *Growth in Partnership,* pp. 94–97.

Chapter 3: Salvation as New Creation

1. Beverly Wildung Harrison, "The New Consciousness of Women: A Socio-Political Resource," *Cross Currents* (Winter 1975), p. 446.

2. Rosemary Radford Ruether, *New Woman, New Earth: Sexist Ideologies and Human Liberation* (New York: Seabury Press, 1975), pp. 210–211.

3. Letty M. Russell, *Growth in Partnership* (see ch. 2, note 9), p. 33.

4. Letty M. Russell, *Becoming Human,* Library of Living Faith (Philadelphia: Westminster Press, 1982), p. 93.

5. Audre Lorde, *Sister Outsider: Essays and Speeches* (New York: Crossing Press, 1984), pp. 111–112. Reprinted by permission of the publisher.

6. Beverly Wildung Harrison, *Making the Connections* (see ch. 1, note 1), pp. 135–138, 141.

7. Ruether, *New Woman, New Earth,* p. 3.

8. Harrison, *Making the Connections,* p. 114.

9. Ibid., p. 86.

10. Ibid., p. 83.

11. Ibid., pp. 145–146.

12. Ibid., p. 149.

13. Speech by Dorothee Soelle at the "Waging Peace" Conference held at Harvard University, Fall 1982.

14. Dorothy Dinnerstein, *The Mermaid and the Minotaur* (New York: Harper & Row, 1976), p. 9.

Chapter 4: Mission: Justice and Solidarity

1. Katie G. Cannon et al., and the Mud Flower Collective, *God's Fierce Whimsy: Christian Feminism and Theological Education* (New York: Pilgrim Press, 1985), p. 33.

2. Letty M. Russell, *The Future of Partnership* (Philadelphia: Westminster Press, 1979), p. 154.

3. Letty M. Russell, ed., *The Liberating Word: A Guide*

to Nonsexist Interpretation of the Bible (Philadelphia: Westminster Press, 1976), p. 16.

4. Letty M. Russell, *Becoming Human* (see ch. 3, note 4), p. 45.

5. Rosemary Radford Ruether, *To Change the World: Christology and Cultural Criticism* (New York: Crossroad Publishing Co., 1981). The book as a whole addresses this question.

6. William Ryan, *Blaming the Victim* (New York: Vintage Books, 1976). This thesis is the major argument of the book.

7. Beverly Wildung Harrison, *Making the Connections* (see ch. 1, note 1), pp. 42–53.

8. Rosemary Radford Ruether, *Disputed Questions: On Being a Christian* (Nashville: Abingdon Press, 1982), p. 92.

9. Russell, *Becoming Human,* pp. 19–21.

10. Marie Augusta Neal, *The Socio-Theology of Letting Go: The Role of a First World Church Facing Third World Peoples* (New York: Paulist Press, 1977).

11. Dorothee Soelle, "Resistance: Toward a First World Theology," *Christianity and Crisis* 39 (July 23, 1979), pp. 178–182.

12. Harrison, *Making the Connections,* p. 28.

13. Rosemary Radford Ruether, *Mary: The Feminine Face of the Church* (Philadelphia: Westminster Press, 1977), p. 80.

14. Harrison, *Making the Connections,* p. 165.

15. Russell, *Becoming Human,* p. 55.

16. Letty M. Russell, "Bread Instead of Stone," *Christian Century* 97 (June 18–24, 1980), pp. 665–669.

17. Harrison, *Making the Connections,* p. 8.

18. Rosemary Radford Ruether, "Foundations of Liberation Languages: Christianity and Revolutionary Movements," *Journal of Religious Thought* 32 (Spring–Summer 1975), p. 80.

19. Harrison, *Making the Connections,* pp. 223–227.

20. Rosemary Radford Ruether, *New Woman, New Earth* (see ch. 3, note 2), p. 31.

21. Letty M. Russell, *Growth in Partnership* (see ch. 2, note 9), p. 39.

22. Russell, *The Future of Partnership,* pp. 106, 110–111.

23. Letty M. Russell, *Christian Education in Mission* (Philadelphia: Westminster Press, 1967), p. 32.

24. Davida Foy Crabtree, "Grandma Gus and Me: History and Politics," *The Drew Gateway* 48 (Spring 1978), p. 40.

25. Alice Hageman, "Sustaining Our Hope," *International Review of Mission* 67 (April 1978), p. 190.

26. Ibid., p. 191.

27. Ibid.

28. Peggy Way, "Homosexual Counseling as a Learning Ministry," *Christianity and Crisis* 37 (May 30 and June 13, 1977), pp. 123–131.

29. Alice Walker, *Goodnight, Willie Lee, I'll See You in the Morning: Poems* (New York: Dial Press, 1979), p. 40.

Chapter 5: Vocation: Meaningful Work

1. Studs Terkel, *Working* (New York: Pantheon Books, 1972), p. xxiv.

2. Beverly Wildung Harrison, *Making the Connections* (see ch. 1, note 1), pp. 48, 52–53.

3. Letty M. Russell, *Becoming Human* (see ch. 3, note 4), p. 15.

4. Harrison, *Making the Connections,* p. 20.

5. Letty M. Russell, *The Future of Partnership* (see ch. 4, note 2), p. 48.

6. Letty M. Russell, *Growth in Partnership* (see ch. 2, note 9), pp. 151–152.

7. See Nancy Chodorow, *The Reproduction of Mothering* (Berkeley: University of California Press, 1978); Carol Gilligan, *In a Different Voice: Psychological Theory and Women's Development* (Cambridge, Mass.: Harvard University Press, 1982).

8. Carter Heyward, *A Priest Forever: The Formation of a Woman and a Priest* (New York: Harper & Row, 1976), pp. 32–33.

9. Harrison, *Making the Connections,* p. 19.

10. They were not significantly different from the sample of Methodist women surveyed in *New Witnesses: United Methodist Clergywomen* by Harry Hale, Jr., Morton King, and Doris Jones (Nashville: United Methodist Church Board of Higher Education and Ministry, 1980), or

the broa̶d̶═════̶cal sample described in *Women of
the Cloth: New Opportunity for the Churches,* by Jackson
Carroll, Barbara Hargrove, and Adair Lummis (San Francisco: Harper & Row, 1983).

11. Rosemary Radford Ruether, *New Woman, New
Earth* (see ch. 3, note 2), p. 70.

12. Ibid., p. 74.

13. Russell, *The Future of Partnership,* p. 138.

14. Alice Hageman, "Sustaining Our Hope" (see ch. 4,
note 25), p. 186.

15. Ibid., p. 184.

16. Russell, *The Future of Partnership,* pp. 132–136.

17. Rosemary Radford Ruether, *Mary* (see ch. 4, note
13), pp. 84–85.

Chapter 6: Feminist Ministry: Vision of Friendship and Solidarity

1. Two books on friendship have recently been pub-
lished: Janice Raymond's *A Passion for Friends: Toward a
Philosophy of Female Affection* (Boston: Beacon Press,
1986) and Mary E. Hunt's *Fierce Tenderness: Toward a
Feminist Theology of Friendship* (New York: Harper &
Row, 1986).

2. Jon Sobrino and Juan Hernandez Pico, *Theology of
Christian Solidarity* (Maryknoll, N.Y.: Orbis Books, 1985),
p. vii. Reprinted by permission of the publisher.